AN APPETITE FOR LIFE

AN APPETITE FOR LIFE
The Education of a Young Diarist
1924-1927

Charles Ritchie

MACMILLAN OF CANADA
A DIVISION OF GAGE PUBLISHING LIMITED
TORONTO, CANADA

Canadian Cataloguing in Publication Data

Ritchie, Charles, 1906-
An appetite for life

(Laurentian library; 68)
ISBN 0-7715-9558-1

I. Ritchie, Charles, 1906-   2. Diplomats –
Canada – Biography. I. Title. II. Series.

FC561.R58A3 1981   327.2′092′4   C81-094671-8
F1034.R58A3 1981

Printed in Canada

First published 1977
First Laurentian Library edition 1981

Macmillan of Canada
A Division of Gage Publishing Limited

To Sylvia

CONTENTS

FOREWORD

The notebooks containing my old diaries are stacked on dusty, toppling piles in the cellar of the apartment house in which I live. They are not, as they should be, arranged in chronological order (a task I have always shirked). After the appearance of my book *The Siren Years,* which covered the years 1937-45, I intended to follow it up with the records of the next decade, and with this object in mind I descended to the cellar in search of those diaries. While pulling notebooks at random from the stacks, I happened to open one much earlier in date than those I was looking for. It was dated September 1924, the beginning of my eighteenth year.

I began to read, and having once started, read on and on. As I did so, an idea struck me. Why not — instead of plodding on with my middle-aged diaries — go back to the youthful ones? The notion appealed to me, yet I realized the risks. Whatever the shortcomings of the later record, it did deal with the worlds of international politics and diplomacy in which by then I moved. It included anecdotes of the famous and the not so famous. If I continued with its publication, I could offer the reader some measure of historical interest, but if I decided in favour of the early diaries, there would be no supporting props of this kind. The youthful diarist would have to stand on his own two feet. Yet in the end I could not resist giving him a chance. It seemed callous to leave him to rot in the cellar when he was plainly longing to get out and tell all.

However, there are limits to one's tolerance of the adolescent ego. To publish the whole of these diaries would be to flood the reader with a spate of words — often repetitious and finally exhausting. So there has had to be a good deal of "culling" — also some telescoping — of the material. This has at times involved the joining up of scenes and episodes originally scattered in fragmentary form over a number of entries. Also, for reasons which will become obvious, names of certain persons have had to be changed.

It is with some trepidation that I introduce my earlier self to the reader in the hope that his company may prove enlivening. For with all his faults and absurdities, he had a great appetite for life, and not least for the comedy of life.

C.R.
Chester, Nova Scotia
June 1977

AN APPETITE FOR LIFE

PART I

HALIFAX
1924-1925

I spent the morning trying to write a short story. I had written some of it last night, and it seemed to flow along as though I were doing "automatic writing". For the first time I thought, "I really can write," capering about my room and saying out loud, "I'm going to be an author!" I wanted to tell someone and went down to the library. Mother and Aunt Millie had not gone to bed yet. They were discussing household finances. I listened to them talking for a few minutes and the impulse to tell them dried up. It is just as well, because this morning when I re-read what I had written I was appalled. It is no good, no bloody good at all. The dialogue is like someone trying to mimic who has got the voice and accent just wrong. As for the story, it stands still. Nothing moves forward and the characters are cardboard.

I crumpled the whole thing up and threw it into the wastepaper basket and took out a new sheet of paper, determined to begin again, but I just stared at the blank page for nearly an hour and nothing happened. Not a thought, not a word came. I found myself looking out of the window at the leaves flittering in the breeze at the edge of the lawn. I watched Aunt Millie come out of the house with her shopping bag over her arm, walking slowly out of sight down the drive. "What is she thinking about?" I wondered; "what she's going to buy for dinner, or about making over last summer's dress, or is she worrying about Eileen's future? She is a mystery, everyone is a mystery. But the characters in my story are not mysteries, they aren't people at all."

I thought I might as well go for a walk as sit here staring into space. I took the short-cut past the stables, over the new bridge, across the railway cutting, through the village, and into the park. It was a funny sort of day. There had been fog but it had lifted, and it was neither hot nor cold. The sun just not out, the tops of the pine trees just moving. I went down to the point where you can look out to sea and sat on a bench. There was a liner

3

moving out of the harbour mouth. It seemed to be moving slowly, hardly at all. The next time I looked it had almost disappeared. I thought, "Oh, to be on board, doing anything, a stowaway, or swabbing the decks, going anywhere. There must be another place different from this. The whole world can't be the same. But what if it turned out to be?" A big raindrop plopped down on my forehead out of the still sky and I turned home. As I walked under the trees in the park the rain came on. I was thinking, "I cannot invent. I shall never, never be a novelist. At the same time, I must write. Why? God knows. So that I'm left with this diary, this useless, drivelling diary. If that is all I have, I had better get on with it."

So little happens to me that is worth recording. No great adventures or tremendous experiences, or passionate love affairs. I know no famous people whom I can describe for posterity. For instance, what has happened today? You may say, "Nothing at all." But something has happened to *me*. I have given up dreaming of being a great writer. That and nothing else, except that we had fried eggs and bacon for breakfast and Georgina, the maid, broke a coffee cup and Aunt Millie said, "Oh, for mercy's sake, that girl again." And Mother said to me, "When you are on your own and have to look after yourself perhaps you'll learn not to throw your clothes in a heap on the floor of the bedroom and just leave them there for someone to pick up." So what am I to write about? I think I will try my hand at describing this house where I live and the people in it. This place is called The Bower and it is on the outskirts of Halifax, Nova Scotia. The tram only goes as far as the corner of Inglis Street, so you have to walk the rest of the way (or we have to, as we have no car). Coming home, you go past the big iron gates at the entrance of Gorsebrook, which is the place adjoining ours, and along beside the stone wall enclosing Gorsebrook's fields and their woods. You turn right beside the dilapidated paling fence enclosing our woods and you come to two squat, square, stone gate-posts and turn into our drive. On the right is the lodge, a little wooden house badly in need of painting, which we let to a family who are behind in the rent. On the left are the barn and the stables where an old Irishman named William Robinson now runs a livery stable and is supposed to look after our furnace in his spare time and when he is sober. The drive winds up on a slight incline under arching trees. On the right there is a meadow sloping down towards the woods. Near the top of the drive you come out onto a square of gravel with the house on one side and lawns and flower beds on the other. The house itself is old, built in 1817, with a Victorian front added later. Its dark-red shingle is overgrown with Virginia creeper. The house seems to slumber away as though nothing had ever disturbed it, but if you go round to the back you get a surprise. Within yards of the kitchen door you are on the edge of a cliff of tawny rock a hundred feet deep; it is the railway cutting. When they put the new railway in it went right through our orchard and so near us that when you see the house from the other side of the cutting it seems almost to be perched on the brink. You can hear the trains rushing and rattling down below and the sound reverberates from the steep rocky sides of the cutting as from the bottom of a canyon. When I was a child and they were still blasting through the solid rock, there would be a siren of warning and crashing dynamite explosions which made the house itself shake. Some people might be bothered by having the cutting so near but it does not worry us in the least, we are so used to it. In fact, I love listening, especially at night when I'm in bed, to the hooting of the engines, the ringing of the cow-bells, the jangling of the couplings, and the sound of the mournful whistle as the trains draw out in the distance, so that I picture them tearing along with their lighted windows through the darkness and dwindling away to the edge of sleep.

When you come into the house through the outside front porch you are in a square hall with two white

5

wooden pillars in the middle. On the walls are portraits, some real ancestors, others, the grander ones, bought by my great-grandfather at a sale, although I like to pretend to myself and sometimes to other people that one of these, a romantic young man wearing a flowered waistcoat, is really a relation of mine. Once someone said they could see a resemblance to me, and I agreed. Fortunately, Mother did not overhear us or I should never have been allowed to forget it. She despises affectation. There is a big fireplace in the hall in which sits a black Franklin stove, not beautiful but giving a lot of heat. The gramophone is on a table by the window. We often roll up the rugs to dance on the parquet floor even if it is not a party but just friends dropping in or people staying.

On the left of the hall is the drawing-room. It is a double room with two fireplaces. It must once have been two rooms. The windows are low, almost on the floor level. One end of the drawing-room is cheerful with chintzes and armchairs; the other end is like an unused parlour. I don't quite know why, except that an upright piano is there and it looks rather neglected as hardly anyone ever plays it. None of my family are musical, although my mother took singing lessons in Dresden when she was a girl but the teacher said her voice lacked something — I cannot remember what. On the right of the hall is the dining-room, which is just a dining-room with red wallpaper and a built-in oak sideboard with knobs and scrolls.

At the end of the hall is the library. This is where we all assemble. There is always someone there, usually several people discussing plans for the day or just talking or sitting about. For this reason it is not a good place for reading, except when Mother reads aloud to us in the evening. I usually read in my own bedroom, taking a book from one of the tall mahogany glass-fronted library bookcases. The glass fronts of the bookcases reflect in the summer the green of the trees outside and in the autumn and winter the firelight. There is a big and very comfortable sofa in front of the fireplace. Mother has her desk by the window. Whenever I think of The Bower I think of this room.

I cannot be bothered describing the upstairs and the bedrooms. There are quite a lot of bedrooms but not so many as you might think considering the number of people who come to stay. There is only one upstairs bathroom and it is very unpopular to stay there any longer than you must.

My own bedroom is sacred to me. In it is the table at which I am writing and looking out of the window at this moment when the sun has just come out and is drying the wet gravel in the drive. I have a small bookcase of my own next my bed in which I keep certain favourite books such as Rupert Brooke's poems in a dark-blue stiff cover with thick deckle-edge pages, Horace Walpole's letters in a limp red-leather binding, some books of my childhood, and whatever novel I am reading or book I am studying for college.

The inhabitants of the house are as follows: My mother, who I shall not attempt to describe as it would be like trying to describe a picture which you are standing too close to. I can see details but I cannot see the whole. Here are a few details. She is a widow. My father, who was much older than she, died nearly ten years ago. I don't know exactly what her age is. I never think of her as being any particular age — probably forty something. I suppose you would say she is handsome rather than beautiful but neither word is quite right. She has the most magnificent dark eyes that can fascinate or scare you depending on her mood. She is generous, compassionate, impatient, and easily bored. She is a born mimic who could imitate anyone. She is a chain-smoker and a terrific tea-drinker. She would do anything for my brother Roley and me and she expects us to achieve something remarkable in life. Roley is away at boarding-school most of the time. He is four years younger than I. When we are together we get on awfully well and can say anything to each other as each knows what the other is feeling.

Aunt Millie and her daughter Eileen live with us and Aunt Millie shares the expenses of the house-keeping. She is not really my aunt but an old friend of Mother's. She is also a widow. Her husband was an Irishman, an officer in the army. He was drowned years ago in an accident. She is fair, and not exactly fat but comfortable. She is placid, sweet-natured, and tactful. Eileen is a few years older than I. I suppose she is about twenty-one. She is fair-haired with brown eyes and a pale skin. Some days she looks beautiful. She was the first love of my life from the age of six till about fourteen. As children we could hardly bear to be apart and, when we were, we wrote each other letters under the assumed names of characters out of books by Baroness Orczy or Stanley Weyman's *Under the Red Robe*. She went to a finishing school in Switzerland and now she is back and it is different. Of course we are still great friends but she is rather critical of me, like an older sister.

Georgina, the maid, comes from Newfoundland. She is young and cheerful. She has an admirer — "my fellow", she calls him. His name is Green and he comes to the house to call for her on her night out. Mother says he is up to no good. The cook is called Mrs. Bright. She is gaunt and old with an immensely deep voice.

Then, of course, there is myself. I am seventeen years old at the moment but will be eighteen next week. By occupation I am a freshman at King's University here in Halifax. I have no character that I know of. I try to be the characters I read about or the people I admire, to enter into their skins and act as they would, but no one notices. They think I am just the same as ever. My main vices are selfishness, vanity, self-consciousness, and talking too much. Also, what the masters at school used to call "impure thoughts", but I don't know if that is a vice or not. I am not altogether lacking in intelligence but I do not care about that. I want to be handsome and dashing and self-assured, but I am angular, beak-nosed, narrow-chested, and wear glasses. I am quite tall, but what is the good of that? I am a compulsive diarist and a greedy reader.

These are the permanent inhabitants of The Bower, but that does not account for the semi-permanent ones, as there always seem to be one or two people staying. Apart from that, the dropping-in is incessant. Never a day passes when I am sitting here like today at my window that I don't see someone or other coming up the drive either in a motor-car or walking, sometimes just for a gossip or a cup of tea, or for no particular reason.

The following will be my diaries for the coming year, beginning January 1, 1925. I want this to be entirely truthful. I am writing because I do not want my life to slip through my fingers like sand.

January 1, 1925

I am in love with a girl called Katherine Akroyd. Or I imagine I am. She has come to be the governess to the Almon children. The Almons are my cousins (I don't believe anyone has as many cousins as I have in this town). They live quite near us, not far from the tram stop in Inglis Street. Katherine is quite young — seventeen. Her family are English. Her father was in the army and they live down in the Annapolis Valley where they have bought a fruit farm which is not doing at all well as they had no experience of fruit-farming. Katherine is as pretty as it is possible to be. She is tall, with a ripping figure. She has a pink and white complexion, adorable nose, grey eyes set wide apart. But that is not all. She goes to your head, to your heart, to every part of you. In herself she is changeable, laughing, teasing, sulking, whatever she pleases. She can twist and turn you round as quick as a flash.

The complication is that Peter is in love with her too, or he says he is. Or is he just playing some kind of game, perhaps to show me that whatever I want he can take

9

easily? Perhaps he can. She seems to prefer his company to mine. I don't altogether blame her. He can always think of something to amuse her or tell her one of his fantastic tales or come to see her with some little joke present. And then, he is better looking than I am, quite handsome in fact. Of course he is only seventeen and I am eighteen and she will be eighteen next month, so Peter is a year behind us. Not that that really helps much.

It is an odd coincidence that we should both be keen on the same girl. He is my only real friend here. I suppose it started when we were both at boarding-school at Trinity College School, Port Hope, and had just come from preparatory school in England and had to take a lot of kidding because of our English accents and were more or less butts for some of the other boys. Peter and his sister Joan are orphans. They live half the time with their English grandmother and half the time with the Archibalds, their Halifax grandparents. Peter, like me, is a freshman at King's. He is a person who believes everything is possible and is full of schemes. He can be very mischievous but he is the best company in the world and would never say no to any adventure. When Miss Akroyd first came here he did not see anything in her, said she couldn't dance well and was not worth the trouble, but strangely enough when he saw that I liked her he began pursuing her, writing her letters and telephoning her all the time and taking her to the movies. Now he claims that he is passionately in love with her. Perhaps he is. I wouldn't wonder if anyone was.

January 5
Took Katherine to the King's College dance. I could see the other boys were surprised to see me with such a pretty girl. She certainly outshone all the other girls and she is so different from them. I overheard Hughie MacDermot say, "Wow! What a figure!", and he came up and asked her for a dance. He is the greatest sheik in college. All the girls are after him. She just looked at her programme,

which was empty except for dances with Peter and me as she doesn't know anyone else at King's, and said, "Come back later. I *might* fit you in somewhere." Of course he did come back and they had one dance.

Although I had most of the dances with Katherine, the evening was not really a success. There are no sitting-out places at King's, just the one room with chairs around the walls where the dancing goes on. It was snowing. You could not go out into the garden, so I never got a chance to be alone with her, and when we were dancing together she was always glancing over my shoulder to see if she was being looked at. If I tried to say anything serious she would toss her head so that her fair hair swung back and just squeeze my hand, or say about some other girl, "Who is that fat fright in green?", or about some boy, "Is he on the football team?" I saw that I was getting nowhere so I tried to be funny. She laughed a lot but I don't know whether she was listening to me or just laughing for laughing's sake. I began to feel quite tired, as if I could never make any headway with her, but when they played the last waltz it was "I'll be loving you always, always". She seemed to melt into my arms and I wished it would go on forever.

When we got back after the dance we walked up and down together outside the Almons' gate. She was quiet and different and said, "I told my sister that I don't know what to make of you." I said, "But it is so simple. I am in love with you." Then I tried to kiss her but she broke away and ran up the Almons' drive, turning to wave goodbye. Although I told her that it was so simple that I was in love with her, I don't know if it is so simple. I don't know just what "being in love" means. Is this what they write and talk about, or is it a concoction of my mind from reading and hearing about love? Yet she is — what is she? I am under her spell.

January 8

Today the sergeant-major has come for the last time, to my great relief. Mother hired him to come twice a week to the house to teach me exercises meant to broaden my chest and strengthen my muscles and make more of a man of me. We repair to my bedroom, I take off my shirt, and he shouts at me, "On your toes! Stick out your chest! Pull in your stomach!", etc., in a voice that could be heard across the barrack square. "One, two, three, down! Up! Up! Down!" He is teaching me breathing exercises, push-ups, squatting exercises, toe-touching. I am supposed to practise these on the days he doesn't come, but all I do is to flail my arms about and take a deep breath when I have come out of my bath. I ignore the rest of them, although the instructions, with a diagram, are stuck up on the wall of my bedroom. When I come down to breakfast Mother asks, "Have you done your exercises?", and I say, "Of course," and she says, "Well, I do hope so, as it isn't worth my going to the expense of paying the man if you don't do the exercises." Of course, she is right, but it is such a fag. She is always after me to ride more often and to work harder. I think she wants me to be a kind of Renaissance man who can do everything from inventing gun-powder to writing sonnets.

January 11

I went down to the stables to see William as Mother had the idea of sending him with an extra horse to bring me back from King's College as the snow is so heavy in the woods that when I walk home that way I am up to my middle in no time. William issued forth from his lair behind the harness room in a very bad temper. He has been on another drinking bout but I gave him the message and he came for me after lectures. It was most embarrassing; a whole lot of the students gathered on the doorstep at King's to watch me mount as no one dreams of riding to college. I had on my heavy overcoat and was carrying all my books under my arm and they were all laughing — I hope with me, not at me — but I felt very self-conscious, so much so that I nearly lost my head and tried to mount on the wrong side of the horse. I suppose the students will be confirmed in thinking me a complete freak. On the way home through the village some of the village boys threw stones at the horses and William called out at them in his Irish brogue, "I'll be after ye; I'll follow ye to the gates of hell." They looked quite scared. Of course they're only small kids. When we got back to the stables I could not help saying to William that I had made a fool of myself before the students by riding back. He said, "You wouldn't be paying attention to a set of jackasses laughing. Are they so ignorant they have never seen a horse in their lives?" This bucked me up considerably.

Peter is living in residence at King's. He got his grandparents to consent. I don't wonder he likes it. When I went up to his room this morning he was still in bed, half-naked, smoking a cigarette at 12:15. His room was in a hell of a mess too. He says no one bothers there and you can do what you like. He says that I should come and join him and that I am suffering from "petticoat government".

January 13
Much talk of money. The family finances seem to be on the rocks. It is not possible for me to go to Oxford while Roley is still at boarding-school — it would be too expensive. Mother says keeping up this place is ruinous. The drive is full of holes and needs new gravel, which costs a lot. Some trees must be cut down before they fall down on our heads. The shutters on the upstairs windows are coming loose. The roof needs to be reshingled, etc., etc.

Sometimes a great wave of selfishness engulfs me. I know how unworthy it is but I feel as though I did not care what happened so long as I get what I want and what I want is to go to Oxford. Professor Walker at King's says that I could get into Oxford at the end of two years at college here as I should have what is called

"Junior Colonial Status". However, it is all a question of money as I should have to have quite a big allowance at Oxford.

January 17

What a nuisance it is that there is only one telephone in this house and that is in the hall so that every word you say can be overheard. I wanted to telephone Katherine just now but Georgina was sweeping the hall and Aunt Millie was filling jam jars in the pantry with the door open. There is no privacy. I had planned what I wanted to say to Katherine when I was in my bath. I wanted to tell her that if she doesn't go with me to the movies to-night all is over between us and that I am not going to spend the whole of my life dangling about after her and listening to her telling me how many boys are in love with her. She is nothing but a brainless flirt anyway.

Later, I did manage to get the telephone to myself this afternoon and spoke to Katherine, but to my surprise she said she supposed *I* was ringing up to get out of taking *her* to the movies, and that she had noticed me the other night making eyes at Muriel Owen and that if I thought her so attractive, why didn't I take her instead if I didn't mind being seen with a girl with a moustache. (Muriel has not got a moustache — only a faint down on her upper lip.)

When I got to the Almons' drive to pick Katherine up to go to the movies, I was surprised to see Peter's car standing there and Katherine and he came down the drive arm in arm, Peter looking like the cat that had swallowed the canary.

All he said was, "We thought it would be more fun if two or three went to the movies together." I was furious, but what could I do. There was no use making a fuss, they would only have laughed, so we all climbed into the front seat of the car and Katherine gave us each a hand to hold and she and Peter chatted away non-stop. I didn't say a word. When we got to the Olympic Movie

Theatre Peter said in lofty tones, "Well, bye-bye children. Enjoy yourselves," and drove off. Katherine said, "You didn't really think he was coming with us, did you? You are silly. It was only a joke. You know I wanted to be alone with you," but I am still not sure that she expected him to drive off like that and leave us together.

Anyway, when we got into the movies she was most affectionate and let me kiss her, but not on the lips, and said, "You know I am very fond of you." I said, "If only we could be together all the time so that we really got to know each other." "But how could we?" she said. "Well," I said, "we could if we were married." She said, "How could we get married, and besides you want to go to Oxford. You would have to take a job if you married me." I said, "I would break stones on the road if I could marry you," but I didn't pursue the subject because I do want to go to Oxford. Still, when we got back to the Almons' drive and were walking up and down, I took off my signet ring and asked her to wear it, explaining that it was only a loan.

January 21

To dinner with Peter's grandparents, the Archibalds. What a gloomy house that is. The dark panelling in the drawing-room and all those dark pictures which Mrs. Archibald says are Rembrandts and then in the small sitting-room there is a green china toad, which is really a spittoon for Mr. Archibald. I am surprised that Mrs. Archibald allows him to keep it there. He is a nice enough old boy but Mrs. Archibald in her shawl is a malicious old woman. I have never forgiven her for telling the dean that she heard that I was odd and lonely and could not get on with the other boys, so that he came and called on my mother to talk of "my case" and advise that I mix more and take more exercise. He sat there with his long red face and his pince-nez and his clerical costume with his legs crossed and I had to come in and sit opposite him while he looked at me through the pince-nez as if I was a specimen in need of prayer. Fortunately, when he was gone, Mother said that she considered his visit an impertinence and wished Mrs. Archibald would mind her own business.

Anyway, Mrs. Archibald went on and on this evening about an article she has written to encourage the speaking of Gaelic in Cape Breton and about her departed father Sir Somebody Something and about the party she gave for the Prince of Wales when he was here. Peter is her favourite and his sister Joan, who is so shy and nice, she does not care a bit about, but Peter amuses her and she can be witty herself — not funny but little needle thrusts. He pushes his luck with her because he is extravagant and in and out of favour. It is an uneasy atmosphere.

January 24
Cousin Reg came out in the afternoon to discuss our finances with my mother as he is a trustee. I could hear them talking in the library. My mother sounded very impassioned and he sounded as though he was trying to soothe her. She wants to make the woods into lots and sell them for houses, but he says the city will never extend in this direction so that no one will come here. She does not respect his opinion but Aunt Millie joins with him to discourage enterprise and to counsel caution. Mother says that my father was always having to find jobs for Cousin Reg, who was his nephew, so she is not impressed by his advice. He is a kind man — a lawyer — wears gold-rimmed glasses on a black silk ribbon round his neck, and puts them on and off his nose when he is nervous. His wife, Cousin Nan, belongs to what is called "the satin set" who drink cocktails all the time and have love affairs with each other. She is a cheerful person — not young, but wears very short skirts, and her hair is dyed different colours at different times. Aunt Millie says she is "bad style". They have a son, Jimmy, who is said to look like me. If anybody says that in my hearing I never forgive

16

them as he has an enormous red nose, pasty complexion, tiny eyes, and a receding chin. Cousin Reg and Cousin Nan think him wonderful but he says about Cousin Reg "t-rust" — he has a terrible stutter — "trust Dad for the platitude". In the evening Mother read aloud to us in the library by the fire, as she has always done and where she has read us all Dickens and Scott and Barrie and Kipling and Conan Doyle. Those are the happiest evenings. She reads so wonderfully fast and does not "put expression" into her voice. I hate it when the telephone rings to interrupt her, but Aunt Millie gets sleepy and fills her hot-water bottle and says "I am for bed" rather apologetically. Tonight she was reading Philip Gibbs's book *Heirs Apparent* about the younger generation in England. Actually it is not such a good book — more like a journalist writing a novel.

January 29
Aunt Lucy and her mother, old Mrs. Cady, have arrived to stay. With Aunt Millie and Eileen and my mother that makes a household of five women. I love Aunt Lucy. She is my favourite aunt, though an adopted one, as she is no real relation. She is the first beautiful woman I ever saw and she's still beautiful, though fatter. Her mother, Mrs. Cady, is old. She is both tall and big, and was once, they say, very handsome. She and Aunt Lucy love gambling, and when they spent the winter in the south of France they lost nearly all their money, which was not much, at the gaming tables, so they are very hard up. Mrs. Cady was a Uniacke before she was married and came from Mount Uniacke, a pillared house by a wooded lake here in Nova Scotia named after the family place in Ireland. She is a funny old girl, likes a joke, believes in ghosts, and wears beaded slippers cut with scissors to relieve her corns.

January 31
Peter has written a love letter to Katherine but so far has had no reply.

In the evening Colonel Almon came out. I admire him because he is so distinguished-looking and such a man of the world and so witty. He makes the most amusing puns. His clothes are beautifully made in London. Much as I admire him, I am not at my ease with him but feel awkward and self-conscious, and fancy he must think me freakish. His wife Cousin Mollie is a very charming person and much easier for me to talk to.

Mrs. Cady is like a naughty child and she will have her say in the conversation, even if it is nothing to do with what is being talked about. If she feels left out, she just snaps her fingers and says, "Fiddledeedee".

February 2
I set off early for King's, walking through our woods. The snow was very deep and it was a cold morning. I got hot climbing in and out of the snow banks. I was thinking quite a lot about Katherine. I don't know how seriously she took me speaking of marriage or how seriously I meant it. My reading about girls in stories and my slight experiments have not really made me sophisticated about them.

When I got to King's, I was summoned before a tribunal of sophomores for wearing spats, which is forbidden to freshmen. The usual penalty is to burn the offender's spats, but they made a concession in my case and only confiscated them for the rest of the term. As a matter of fact they weren't mine at all but only an old pair that Peter had lent me.

After lectures I ran into Professor Walker in the corridor. He said that he had met all the most brilliant men in Nova Scotia and that they did not amount to a row of ninepins and that all this bunkum about King's College being an ancient institution was tiresome drivel. Of course, he is an Oxford man and very brilliant, but I think he was just letting off steam.

A man gave a lecture tonight at King's on sex which was unpleasant but rather amusing. He had diagrams, but I could never learn to do anything from a diagram. The lecturer was quite old and had a terrible cold. Peter and I walked back from the lecture with Cyril, who announced that he intended to keep pure until he was married. Then he had the nerve to say that he had never in his life masturbated, which was too much for Peter and me. We told him he should see a doctor at once because there must be something wrong with him and he said, "Not at all. I just do not choose to pamper myself."

This evening I read Oscar Wilde's essays *Intentions*, which have made me feel what the beauty of life could be, and his *De Profundis* has had a spiritualizing influence on me. Professor Walker in his lecture yesterday spoke of "the spirit that makes so many of us at eighteen go about patting ourselves on the chests and saying that we are atheists." He said he had been through that phase himself but that one grew older and realized the necessity for revealed faith. I hope I am not an atheist. I certainly don't feel like patting myself on the chest, but I have little faith.

This evening I had a discussion about my future with my mother. I do dread these discussions of my future.

She began by asking "what I thought of doing as an occupation after college." I said, "I should like to be an author but I haven't got the talent." She said, "Even if you have talent you can't earn your living like that; you must have some profession. I know you don't want to go in for the law like your father, and you don't want to go into a bank, and you don't want to go into the Army, but what *do* you want to do? I'll back you to the hilt if I know what your ambition is. You know that." "Well," I said, "I want to go to Oxford and then perhaps into the diplomatic service," and she said, "Where do you think the money is coming from? You have to have a big allowance in the diplomatic service. I don't know where you get these grand ideas." It was on the tip of my tongue to answer, "I get them from you," but fortunately I said nothing.

All the same it is not fair. Sometimes Mother paints such pictures of my future, saying I should get out of this place and live in the great world and meet interesting people, and then in the next breath she says it is all impossible. One day she puts ideas in my head and in the next she wipes them out. Of course it is all a matter of money. She wants me to have what I want but we cannot afford it. When I stagger up to my room after one of these sessions about my future I fall into bed and sleep as if I were drugged.

All this talk about the future, my future. How do I know I'll be alive this time next year? I may die young like Meisner at King's who died of pneumonia last year, just my age. I don't mind dying all that much. I often think of it. There could be a lot worse things, only I don't feel that I will die. That seems to be something that happens to other people. No, I shall go on and on as a bank clerk in a small town, and take to drink like so many of my family, and day after day write this damned diary about nothing, and Nothing will be my name.

February 7
Lord Curzon is dead. In her memoirs Mrs. Asquith says that his face had an expression of "enamelled self-assurance". How I wish my face had.

I took a walk with dog and stick in the woods and in Gorsebrook fields and went down to the stables to see William, who has been drunk for two days. He looked very yellow and was very bad-tempered, saying how clumsy I was and would never be any good at riding unless I rode every day. But of course, as our stables are now livery stables he gets paid when we ride, except that Mother says he owes us so much for the rent that the only way to get it out of him is to ride every day. He is supposed to look after the furnace in the house too and has not done so lately, so that it went out. I helped him feed the horses. He railed against Mrs. Mulroney, who has been so kind to him and helped him financially. He says she does not know "a bee from a bull's foot about horses". I enjoy being with William. He is a human being and never makes me feel self-conscious.

Mother would like to convert the lodge into a pretty small house and offered it to Mrs. G., but she replied, "We may be hard up, but not to the point of living at your lodge gates." Mother says she is a silly ass.

February 9
I dreamed of Katherine last night. Her body was beside me in bed, her lips on mine. When I got up and went to the window all I could see was a patch of gravel glistening wetly. The lawn and the flower beds and the big maple tree in front of the house were all blotted out by motionless, silent fog, and I could taste the salty taste of the fog as I leant out of the window. I could hear Georgina banging about in the kitchen, so I got dressed and went down and got her to give me a cup of coffee and decided to go for a walk in the park before breakfast. The fog was so thick that crossing the bridge over the railway cutting I couldn't see the train that was rumbling and jangling past below me under the bridge. In the park the trees were dripping. I was the only living thing about except for a few scuttling squirrels. I felt weightless and empty, drained by my dream. I thought, I don't love Katherine now, and it seemed worse than her not loving me.

February 12
In the afternoon I went to call on the Ritchie cousins, Ella, Eliza, and George. They have to be wound up like toys to talk and then Ella and Eliza both talk at once, while the bearded George sits by the window smoking Egyptian cigarettes and snorting occasionally; he never speaks. Cousin Ella is nearly eighty and Eliza a little younger. They used to live at Winnick on the Northwest

Arm until their coachman burned down the house in a fit of spite. Their father was my great-uncle John and his wife was an Almon. In that generation four Ritchie brothers and one Ritchie sister all married Almons, who were their first cousins, and they had been brought up together. My mother says it was almost incestuous and so unenterprising. Ella and Eliza go to Europe every year to visit the art galleries, which I don't think George enjoys much. Their clothes are the same as they were forty years ago. They can only find them in one dress shop in London. There was another sister who married. It was considered an "unsuitable" marriage, but when she was only seventeen she had encouraged this suitor and when she wanted to get out of it her father said, "A Ritchie's word is as good as his bond. If you said yes you must abide by it." She walked out in the snow in her nightdress in the middle of winter, hoping she would catch pneumonia and die rather than marry him, but she did not die and she did marry him.

February 13
Lent begins next week and I intend to bring into force a new Lenten regime of work and efficiency. Every waking moment will be accounted for by the system. Also I shall save money. That part will not be difficult as I haven't got any to save. All my money is spent and I owe Peter. My allowance of $5 a month is not enough. All the other boys have more but I cannot say this to Mother as I know how hard up we are for ready cash.

Of course Peter has a car and we haven't, but I don't care — I don't want a car anyway. I went into town with him today. He was wearing a new grey fedora with the brim turned down and smoking a pipe, which is a new development. We wandered about the stores feeling very superior and then went into The Green Lantern for milkshakes from the new pretty waitress and went to a ripping movie called "The Perfect Flapper". I got home to find a lot of people here: one group playing mah-jong, another bridge, and some dancing to the gramophone in the hall. Major Uniacke was among them, Aunt Lucy's cousin and admirer — he had "drink taken" and was very funny and nice. He and Aunt Lucy talk to each other by the hour. What about?

As the people here tonight were all older I went up to bed early and read a book on Australia by Bryce. I do hope I shall never have to go to Australia.

February 15
At breakfast Georgina, the maid, put before me a plate of porridge with a pair of scissors in it. She really is getting too queer for words.

Tonight was the night of the Dalhousie dance. I took Katherine, who promised me or half promised me four dances, but she danced three of them with Bill Macaulay, who she is determined to enslave although he is only an overgrown schoolboy. During our one dance I asked her to return my ring and said that from now on everything was completely over between us. She hardly bothered to listen. Finally I was so fed up that I started dancing with Sue Maloney and she pressed up against me and we went out to her car and we sat or rather lay on the back seat and she let me do almost everything. I had a good time of a sort but I kept thinking of that brainless flirt, Katherine, dancing with Bill, and she happened to look so damnably pretty tonight. When I got out of Sue's fleshy embraces I felt disgusted with myself and her. I should feel grateful to her. She is a kind creature and Katherine is far from kind. The only consolation is that Peter had just as rotten a time as I had. He took Miss Henderson, who is supposed to be ultra-respectable, but she spent five dances in a car with the Pemberton boy and Peter had to dance with his sister.

I invited Sue to go to the movies with me next week. She is quite attractive in a way.

Mother and Aunt Lucy had an argument about religion at breakfast. Mother is the most wonderful woman in the world but her arguing methods would enrage a saint. She said she was going to ask Mr. Logan to dinner tomorrow. He seems quite devoted to her but I consider him a bore, especially as she unwisely said to me that she thought he would be a "good influence" for me. Who wants a good influence?

I walked to King's along the railway cutting, which saves time, instead of going through the woods, and I like it. I am the only one who walks there along between shining railway lines, shut in on either side by the high cliffs of rock and then under the spanning bridge. I meet no one and so I do not have to compose my face into the right expression as one has to do passing people in the street.

There was a talk today at King's from a Northwest policeman about Mount Everest. He was a fine man but a damned dull speaker. I walked home with Mr. Wilmot, an Englishman with a beautiful white moustache. He told me things about our jails here; the filth and corruption and misery that go on in them remind one of descriptions of eighteenth-century prisons. A maniac of seventy is put in the same cell as a boy of fourteen. Mr. Wilmot spoke to the Attorney-General about it and all he said was, "The bloody buggers all need their necks stretched." How disgusting to think that all this is going on under our noses and nobody cares except Mr. Wilmot. Hearing this took me out of myself — a rare occurrence. I went back to tea with the Wilmots. Mrs. Wilmot is rather a formidable lady. I sat on a seat made from elephant tusks and talked incessantly. The Wilmots have a niece staying with them whose father and mother were killed in a train accident. She is called Miss Ferguson and is peculiarly plain and fat and wears glasses cut in shape like a pie-crust table. She told us about California where her family lived and how much more friendly the people are there than here. She said she didn't expect a boy to spend money on taking her out but would be quite happy to go for a walk in the woods. That is one walk I do not intend to take.

February 21
I walked into town in the rain wearing my new Oxford bags and my brown tweed coat, smoking a cigarette as I went, feeling very jaunty. I stopped off at the Almons' en route to have a chat with Katherine, although I had been talking to her on the telephone half an hour earlier. She was sitting on the steps wrapped up in a rug as if on a sea voyage — pale and silent and looking quite plain. When she is like this I love her all the more.

Passing the Roman Catholic cathedral I thought I would go in as I have never seen the interior. I hoped no one would see me going in as they might think I had been "converted", but once inside I felt a sensation of calm and peace as if I could pray here if I knew what to pray for. I sat on one of the back seats for nearly an hour. There was no service going on, just one or two old women on their knees and the stillness of the crimson lamps flickering.

February 22
In the morning I read some Hegel for my political science course. I hate Hegel when I understand him. How can one compare him with a thinker like Spinoza, who is so lucid, or with St. Thomas Aquinas. Hegel and algebra . . . what a diet!

Today at tea-time a horrible Englishman came to call on us. He is in the cable ship and said he had some kind of letter of introduction to Mother. The minute he came into the hall he looked around at the portraits and said, "What jolly ancestors." No one knew what to say. Then at tea he began saying to Aunt Millie, "Of course you know Lady X or Lord Y," and each time she said she didn't, so he switched onto the subject of the Jews, and a

25

book called *The Protocols of Zion*, which showed that there was a Jewish conspiracy to undermine all institutions and how they sacrificed Christian babies in secret. Mother got more and more impatient and finally said, "That's all stuff and nonsense," so he shut up. I don't think he'll come back in a hurry. When he had gone Mother said, "There's nothing nicer than an English gentleman but nothing worse than that kind of third-rate Englishman. They should not be allowed to come out here. They do so much harm to the Empire."

February 25
When I came out of the barber shop today who should I see come strolling down the street but Peter, wearing his new grey fedora, a grey suit, and grey spats, and smoking his pipe. We walked back together to the Archibald house. His grandparents were out. Peter said to me, "How about a drop of whisky?", so we went into the dining-room and helped ourselves out of the decanter on the sideboard. I said, "Won't your grandfather notice that there is less in the decanter?" Peter said, "We could fill it up with water," so we did, although I have always been told that that was the unforgivable sin. Then we went into the sitting-room and Peter began talking about going to Cambridge, which he expects to do next autumn, and of the adventures that he and I would have when he was at Cambridge, how we would conquer Mayfair, and shine in the fashionable world, and meet beautiful women like the heroine of Michael Arlen's *The Green Hat*, and how different it would all be from our dull life in Halifax. Then he told me about all the trouble he is having with his grandparents. He says he is quite out of favour. His grandmother complains all the time about his being extravagant and coming in at all hours and not working hard enough. Poor Peter, why can't parents and grandparents get it through their heads that we are now grown up and not schoolboys any longer? Peter was at his nicest today and I felt so fond of him, but just as I was

leaving he couldn't resist telling me that Katherine had telephoned him and said that I was annoyed with her but that she could make me come around any time she wanted to. This made me feel quite sick, disgusted with Katherine and with Peter for telling me, and, most of all, with myself for being such a damned fool as to be taken in by her.

February 26
In the morning Mrs. Cady noticed in the paper the death of Admiral C. Mother was a little upset . . . not much. I remember the summer when I was fifteen when he was in love with her and used to come to the house so often when he was in command of the fleet here. He was a cheery old boy with poppy eyes, very kind to Roley and me. He owned an ancient castle in England and wanted Mother to marry him but unfortunately he had a wife already, but he said he thought she would give him a divorce. Mother never took him seriously, but she did write to a friend in Bermuda to find out whether he had gone about proposing to women when he was in command there and the answer was, "Nothing of the sort," so she thought that at any rate he was in earnest, which pleased her.

March 1
I have very few friends here, I mean friends of my own age, apart from Peter. Of course, there are lots of people about the house always and I am not at all lonely, but I can't seem to get on with my fellow students at King's. I am afraid they think I am affected or stuck up, when I want to be accepted by them, but I can't seem to put a foot right, and the harder I try the worse it gets. For instance, last summer we were all swimming in the Northwest Arm and three or four of the boys were lying sunning themselves on the wharf in their bathing suits, including Fabian and Harry and Dick, and I climbed out of the water and up the ladder to join them. They

were talking among themselves but when I appeared they shut up. I made some joking remark but no one replied. They made me nervous, with the unfortunate result that I went on talking and the silence continued. I wished I could escape but I seemed rooted to the spot. Finally, with a supreme effort, I got to my feet and said as nonchalantly as I could manage, "Well, I must be going. I didn't realize it was so late." Dick just raised his arm in a kind of mute gesture and when I got back to the bathing hut I heard a shout of laughter. I shall never forget the humiliation I felt. Every time I go into that hut the smell of the wet wooden floor where people have thrown off their bathing suits brings that moment back to me. Yet perhaps it was my imagination and they were just sleepy from swimming and then someone made a joke that had nothing to do with me . . . but I delude myself . . . Peter has told me that the students at King's laugh at me.

I dropped in to see Cousins Ella and Eliza this afternoon. Cousin Ella is a nineteenth-century Whig in politics; Macaulay is her gospel. Eliza, when she was a younger girl, I suppose about 1870, went off to Cornell University to study Sanskrit when no girl in Nova Scotia had ever been to a university. What is more, she announced she was an atheist, which shocked her evangelical family. She once told me that being an atheist "was like coming out of a darkened room into the light of day." She should be more interesting to talk to than she is but her conversation is mostly dry pebbles. She and Ella are tremendous self-scratchers. When Ella was talking today she nearly tore her necklace to pieces with clawing at it. When Eliza gave a lecture last term at Dalhousie on Sanskrit she scratched herself all the time in her most intimate parts. It was quite embarrassing but she was unconscious of it.

Walked to town in the rain in my brown tweeds with the coat collar turned up, smoking a cigarette, when I ought to have stayed at home working at algebra. If I do not do some study work at algebra, I shall never pass the examination, which I have failed twice already. The trouble is that I don't really understand why "X" should equal anything. No one has ever been able to get through my head the idea behind algebra. I am being tutored by dear old Miss Stewart and I pretend to understand when she explains out of politeness, so she always thinks I will do well in the exam and is surprised when I fail.

March 15
The visiting Professor of English is a po-faced ignoramus with bristling hair like steel filings. I walked back with him after a lecture today and happened to mention Rupert Brooke. He said, "That is the man who wrote 'In Flanders' Field the poppies grow'. I haven't read much of his stuff." I was too dumbfounded by his ignorance for utterance. Also he considers Swinburne to be "unhealthy". His lecture was about nature poets: the birds and the bees and the pretty flowers, that sort of stuff. It is a scandal that he knows nothing of Rupert Brooke, that wonderful poet. When I got home I took the volume of his poems out of the bookshelves and began to read it through again, although I know most of them almost by heart. Then I copied out the sonnet that begins: "Oh death will find me, long before I tire of watching you", and ends: "Toss your brown delightful head amusedly among the ancient dead". I decided to send it to Katherine. Of course her hair is yellow and not brown. I felt such an ache of longing for her that it hurt like a real ordinary pain, then I thought I can't go on mooning about like this. I must do some work. The geometry test is next week and this time I *must* pass. Oh, the torment of maths. Will I never be delivered from them, and what is the use of them? What has an isosceles triangle got to do with me, and why the hell do I care what the squares equal?

Still, I had just settled down to work when I looked out of the window and there walking up the drive was Katherine herself with the two little girls. She was wearing a pale pink dress and swinging a straw hat on her arm, coming out of the green tunnel of the trees in to the sunlight onto the gravel in front of the house. I called out to her and she looked up at my window, tossing back her hair like the girl in the sonnet. I went down to talk to her. We sat together on the porch steps in the sun while the children played on the lawn, pretending they were horses. She said, "I was so surprised to find you in" (although she knows perfectly well that I never go to lectures on Tuesday). I gave her an envelope with the poem in it but asked her not to open it till she got home. She said, "Take your specs off and let me look at your eyes. You look quite different without specs, like another person. Put them on again." I said, "You have my ring and I haven't got anything of yours," so she said, "You can have this hankie if you like," and she gave me a tiny handkerchief smelling of that lily-of-the-valley scent she uses. I asked her if she really knew how much I loved her and she said, "I suppose you say that to all the girls." I could have hit her. She spoils everything by pretending not to understand. Then she began calling to the children, who were playing perfectly contentedly, and they came running up and asking questions, so I said, "I must get back to work but I will walk with you down the drive." She let me take her arm. It was like a piece of wood. She made herself so unresponsive and looked so sulky, I said, "When will I see you again?", and she said, "Oh, I don't know. I am going to the movies with Peter tonight and I'm busy all day tomorrow." So we parted at the lodge gates and she didn't even turn round to say goodbye but bent down with her back to me and began fussing with little Lale's hair and kissing her. She says she doesn't know what to make of me, but I certainly don't know what to make of her. Does she love me even an inch, or is this all a game?

March 16

I got a very sweet note from Katherine this morning saying that she loves the poem and that she never had a
poem written to her before and that she had shown it to
her sister, who said how beautiful it was. Then it dawned
on me that she thinks I wrote the poem myself as I didn't
put Rupert Brooke's name to it. It had never occurred to
me that she would think this, especially as last month I
lent her my copy of Rupert Brooke's poems and she said
how much she enjoyed them, but I can't explain to her
now that I didn't write it. It would spoil everything.

I am going to take up fencing. Rodney Wilmot has
talked me into it and I am to go three times a week to the
Dalhousie gymnasium starting tomorrow.

I had decided last week that I would intervene in the
college debate on the future of India despite the fact that
I know nothing whatsoever about India, but I could not
know any less than that stupid dolt Anderson who has
been holding the floor on the subject. I felt very nervous
beforehand and went over my speech walking up and
down in my bedroom about a hundred times. Then I tore
up my notes and threw them in the wastepaper basket as
I despise reading a speech from notes. All the way to
King's along the railway cutting I was sweating, really
sweating, with the fear that I was going to make a fool of
myself, but the moment I got to my feet my self-consciousness vanished. I felt as though I were on the stage,
not myself but another person, quite at my ease. In my
speech I argued that India should remain under British
rule, that it would be worse off free than it is now. I chose
this line because Anderson was bleating about freedom.
Professor Walker said afterwards that he disagreed with
everything I said but that it was an exceptional speech
and that I had a great future before me.

March 19

Georgina, the maid, is somewhat peculiar. Three times
this week she has stepped on the bell on the floor under

31

the dining-room table and then rushed to the front door to open it, thinking it was the doorbell ringing. You would think that by now she would have caught on to the fact that the dining-room bell rings in the kitchen. Perhaps she is thinking of her "fellow". Yesterday she was trying to decide what to wear to go out with him and she said, "I guess I look better into a tam-o'-shanter than I look into anything else."

Wouldn't it be nice if for one day and night I could stop thinking of sex. I wonder if other people think of that one subject as often as I do, and not only thinking it. I sometimes wonder whether I am a bit crazy and this spring weather makes it worse. What would it be like to be castrated? A jolly good idea I should think, then I could concentrate on my work, pass my exams, save money, and have a brilliant career. People say that playing games takes your mind off it: "A healthy mind in a healthy body" and all that stuff. Certainly I don't think fencing will make much difference. Anyway I have not got a healthy mind and I am not sure that I want to have one.

I went for my first day's fencing today. It is quite hard work. The first thing I had to learn was to keep my arm straight as everything is done with the wrist and I began by lunging about the way I have seen duels in the movies.

March 24
I devoted the whole day to my thesis on government and my head whirls with town councils and municipal by-laws.

Today our cat was chloroformed out of mistaken kindness because her leg was broken. I knew her better than anyone and I am sure she was still interested in life.

In the evening old Mrs. Cady began talking about her youth. Her father, although the eldest son, was an impoverished clergyman, so he gave up Mount Uniacke to his brother. Then all her family of seven went to live in a tiny house in Halifax. Her uncle, Norman Uniacke, was eccentric. Even in the daytime he always wore a red cotton night-cap and a long dustcoat. My mother said that once when she was a child visiting them he passed through the drawing-room carrying a pot of boiling water and she asked what he was going to do with it and he said, "If you must know, child, I am going to wash my buttocks."

March 30
Mother has started raking the gravel in front of the house, which is a very bad sign as it shows she is bored and impatient — sick of having all these people in the house. She gets these spurts of energy and sometimes cleans and polishes all the shoes in the house. On the other hand, she cannot cook an egg and never goes near the kitchen if she can help it.

April 2
I spent the morning at the polling booth as a volunteer helper for the elections. The voting took place in a big wooden shed. I had to rush about with cards with electors' names on them. Meanwhile, motor-cars were being sent out in all directions to bring in voters who had no other way of getting here. We heard later in the day that the Conservatives had made a clean sweep, which was very satisfactory. Of course, the family have always been Conservatives and so I am, though I don't know much about politics. Also, all our friends and relations are very much against the Americans. Mr. Whitman says he would "prefer even the Russian Communists to Americans", and he is the most conservative person I know. As for Cousin Susie, when her sister's child died (she had married an American) Susie said, "Well, it is sad, of course, that he died, but if he had lived he would have grown up an American," but then she is a bit crazy on the subject of our Loyalist ancestry as if the American Revolution had happened yesterday. What we all believe in is the Empire, but my father, when he was alive, be-

lieved in Canada, and my great-uncle John was what they call a Father of Confederation. My mother's family were against Confederation and wanted Nova Scotia to be on its own as part of the Empire. I find it hard to think of Canada. It is so enormous, all those prairies and mountains and cities and open spaces. Nova Scotia is small enough to understand and even when I want to get away from it I know it is my country and I can't do anything about that even if I wanted to.

Reading Swinburne's *Mary Stuart* all morning when I should have been preparing for my mathematics exam. Mother's favourites are Byron and Keats in poetry and Scott in prose, but Swinburne is my discovery. The colour and music carry me into an enchanted haze. I am reading Chastelard's *Love for the Queen*. It is the most sensuous poetry I have ever read. I am waiting for a girl on whom I shall hang Chastelard's passionate words and be ready to die for her.

Cousin Reg came to tea today. He is a kind man, but what hell it would be if my mother died and he became my guardian.

April 4
I do not believe that Peter is the least in love with Katherine. That is all put on, partly to show off and partly to tease me. I expect he does like kissing her, etc. — who wouldn't — but he doesn't love her. All the same, he gets further with her in some ways than I do just because he really doesn't give a damn and she knows it.

We were just starting out today for little Lale Almon's birthday party when who should arrive but Cyril in a very lachrymose mood and began talking religion. He started on the evangelicals and the Low Church in general, how narrow and ignorant they are, and then Mother came in and said to hurry up to be at the Almons' on time, and Cyril went right on about Christ's death being blood sacrifice and that auricular confession is sanctioned in the prayer book, until Mother exploded with irritation and practically shooed him out of the house. He couldn't have chosen a worse subject, especially in Mother's mood in the last few days, and as she always particularly disapproves of the notion of blood sacrifices and is not at all in favour of confession, auricular or otherwise.

April 5
Mother continues in a very irritable mood. I think it is all these people who infest the house for lunch, tea, and dinner. Yet she makes them all welcome and in fact is really quite glad to see them and charms them with her interest in them and her warmth of welcome. But then she gets bored, and when they have gone her mimicry of them is merciless. Yet if they were in trouble there is nothing she would not do for them. She expects more out of life than it offers and so do I.

I went into Miss Stewart's for tutoring in maths. I would rather break both my legs than face the algebra paper. As I was walking into town wearing my new beige-coloured Oxford bags some village boys followed me along, calling out names. I turned round on them and told them to shut up. At first they looked quite abashed but the minute my back was turned they began again, one red-headed boy imitating the way I was walking and pretending to smoke a cigarette. To throw them off my tracks I went in by the gate to the Gorsebrook field but they leant over the stone wall and kept on calling. I walked slowly through the field trying to seem unconcerned and not to hurry in case they would think I was running away from them. It was a most humiliating experience. Is this going to happen every time I go out of our gates, and wouldn't it be awful if it happened while I was walking with Katherine?

Dear old Miss Stewart thinks I will pass the exam but she is wrong. She loves mathematics the way I love reading. She is a fine person, a high-minded Scotswoman, endlessly patient, wears an old-fashioned black silk blouse, with glasses that snap on an attachment on her

35

breast, and has white hair done up into a bun. As I walked home I thought that everyone was looking at me as though I were peculiar. When I got home Mrs. Fitzgerald was here for tea — she has goitre, one eye gone and the other very much popped out — also an Englishwoman, whose name I forget, who said that she feared that a play she and her young son had seen "would put *certain* ideas into his head and *in that way* she did not like the play." Quite a good tea but the chocolate cake was stale.

Cyril joined us at tea. He says the new curate "is so good with fallen women and that the Dean would horsewhip them."

Professor Falconer talked to me after lectures today. He is a splendid person, so cultivated and civilized and calm. He seems miles away from me. How do people get to be so calm? I want to do so infinitely much, read so much and write so much, and love and travel and adventure.

April 15

I took my algebra exam today in that great bare gymnasium-like room that I know too well. There were five problems to solve in two hours. My brain seemed to seize up like a car does. Instead of thinking of the problems I kept thinking: what if I fail as I have done three times before? How disappointed Miss Stewart will be after all her work.

April 17

The Fleet is in. What a day! Peter and I were invited aboard and taken into the wardroom and each had a tremendously potent cocktail and heard some wonderfully funny stores, quite unprintable.

Then in the evening to the much-talked-of Government House ball for the Navy. I did not enjoy it as much as I hoped as I danced mostly with Sue, who wore a pale green dress and had a bad toothache. Government House has been redecorated and lost all its old-fashioned atmosphere. The ballroom looks like a hotel or the saloon of a liner. I was getting quite tired, especially as from vanity I had not worn my glasses, when an extraordinary thing happened. There was a most stunningly beautiful girl there, an American from out of town, just like a movie star, wearing a sequined dress, very close-fitting to her figure. All the naval officers were after her, waiting in rows to dance with her, so I thought, "Oh well, I'll have a try," so I went to the buffet and drank two glasses of champagne in quick succession and then I went up to her when she was dancing with a senior Navy man and tapped him on the arm and said, "May I cut in, please?" He looked quite astonished but she said, "Why not," and swayed out of his arms into mine. We danced a few steps and she said, "I am tired of dancing; let's go into the garden," so we did. The garden was dark apart from a few coloured lanterns strung up and we stood side by side, looking over the harbour with its glimmering lights. Then she suddenly turned round and kissed me full in the mouth. *Such* a kiss. I was stunned with surprise and absolute delight. Then she said, "I suppose we must go back to that boring dance." As we walked up the stone steps leading into the hall she kissed me again and put her body against mine and whispered, "You are a sweet kid." When we got back into the lighted ballroom there were the Navy men waiting for her and she blew me a kiss and danced away. Sue said, "Who was that American girl you were dancing with? She's drunk." She may have been a little, but nothing can take away from the fact that the most attractive girl at the whole ball kissed me of her own accord.

April 18
I have accepted a part in the college play. There were rehearsals all morning. It is a Booth Tarkington comedy called *Tweedles*, very whimsical and not very comic but "clean fun", suitable for the audiences we are likely to

have in the small towns where we hope to raise money for King's University, which is perennially broke. It is planned that wherever possible the members of the company will be put up by well-wishers of King's, often the Anglican clergyman and his wife or a lady church-worker. My part in the play is that of the heroine's rich uncle, a gruff old codger who turns out in the end to have a heart of gold. At first he opposes the girl's marriage on the ground that the hero, who comes off the farm, is not good enough to marry his beautiful niece and future heiress. In order to underline my wealth and social status I am condemned to wear a morning coat throughout the play and am made up with what appears to be putty-coloured butter in which are drawn lines to indicate my wrinkles. I wear a very hot and heavy horsehair wig and a white handlebar moustache which so far cannot be made to stick properly. I carry a cane and hobble about the stage with bent back, wheezing and chuckling in what I hope is an old-mannish manner, although I have never met an old man who was at all like my version. All the actors and actresses are students at King's. The heroine is acted by Alice Prouse. She comes from Newfoundland, has fair hair, a very pale complexion, light blue eyes, and a rather long nose. I think she is definitely attractive. The hero is played by Malcolm Dymock. He is a second-year student, handsome in a heavy way, with disgustingly wavy blond hair, and is much too pleased with himself. The clergyman who finally weds the happy couple is acted by Henry Ross, a charming, humorous character. The only thing I have against him is that his ambition in real life is to be a schoolmaster. My counterpart, the hero's farmer father, is Max. I went to school with him and have always liked him, although we could not be more different. He never reads a book and is interested only in sport and girls. He drinks quite a lot and is deaf in one ear. Then there is Hunter, also a second-year student. He is supposed to be the "business manager" of the company. He is a most peculiar character and if I had a business I would not like him to manage it. He is dirty, ugly, and aggressive. There are two other girls in minor parts: Miss Sullivan, who takes offence readily but is quite fun if she lets herself go, and Miss Caducci, who is pale, composed, and intelligent. The girls are under the chaperonage of Mrs. Macrae, who will accompany the tour. She used to be Dean of Women at the college and looks, as P. G. Wodehouse would put it, "like a sheep who has had bad news". She is fussy and ineffectual and revels in getting one aside and confiding, or being confided in. Her hair is her great problem. She is always doing it up in different ways but it never stays because she says "It is too fine".

April 20
Our tour has begun. The whole company packed into the train to go to Windsor. We went straight to the theatre for rehearsals only to find that there was no stage furniture as the manager had made no arrangements for it. I can see that this is going to be a problem throughout the tour. We have our own stage sets but no furniture and will have to borrow from well-wishers in the towns. I felt nervous all day at having to be on stage for the first time. I lunched at King's Collegiate, the first of the many boarding-schools I have attended in my life. Roley was only eight years old when he went there. Today we ate in the school dining-room but at a table apart from the boys with the headmaster and his sister, Miss Judd. The headmaster was just the same, or rather he was the same as he always used to be with visiting grown-ups, quite different from when you were waiting to be beaten by him, or when he came swirling through the halls of the school with his black gown flying. He seems a nice little man and you wonder what you were frightened of. Miss Judd still keeps the art of making you feel uneasy. I suppose it is a habit she formed to deal with the boys. She kept talking of how untidy I was as a boy and how my glasses used to be done up with string, and repeated the jokes the ser-

geant-major used to make about my performances on the bar in the gym, saying that it was "better to watch Ritchie major on the bar than to watch Charlie Chaplin". I felt as if at any moment I might be bewitched back into being one of the grubby little boys at the long tables and would never be able to escape, and that my being grown-up was a kind of dream. I could hardly believe my ears when, as I was leaving, the boy who was detailed to show us to the door called me "Sir".

The play went quite well. There was a lot of clapping and some laughter. I was not so nervous once the curtain went up. The only trouble was with my moustache which kept slipping off.

April 21
Charlottetown where we arrived today is an exceptionally dusty place and we got a very dusty welcome from a local clergyman, an Englishman with a ponderous jowl and a canonical manner. He took us to the Rectory, but only for tea, although it was quite a big house and he could have put us up, or at least offered us a meal. He has a selfish-looking wife, who kept on a sort of pink boudoir cap during tea, and three daughters, one slightly cross-eyed. He had made no arrangements as to where we were to stay, and Ross and I had to search around for ourselves till we found this boarding-house which stinks of stale whisky. Females kept appearing and disappearing in the hall. After supper I went out onto the hotel verandah and got into conversation with a stoutish gentleman who was smoking a cigar and rocking to and fro in one of the hotel rocking-chairs. I sat down beside him. He turned out to be a salesman for Eversharp pencils. I remarked that this seemed to be a pretty lousy kind of boarding-house and he said, "Oh, there are compensations." I asked him what he meant and he laughed and said, "Well, it isn't for me to tell you if you don't know, but it is more of a bawdy-house than a boarding-house." I was going back to break the news to Ross, with whom I

was sharing a room, when in the hall a woman stopped me and said, "Hey kid, want to come and listen to my gramophone records later on? It'll only cost you two bucks. It's the third room down the hall." I could not see her well in the half light except that she was a woman, not a girl, quite plump, with dark eyes. After Ross and I had gone to bed, I got restless and said, "You know, I think I'll try and see what it's like." He said, "I shouldn't if I were you," but I put on my trousers and went down the hall to her room, knocked, and went in. She was lying on her bed reading a comic paper but she looked up and said, "I thought you might be coming around." Then she put on the gramophone and without further ado began to undress. She did not turn out the overhead light and then I saw that she was really old, I mean at least thirty, and when she smiled her mouth was full of gold teeth. My heart and everything else sank. She said, "Cheer up, it'll soon be Christmas. Why don't you take your pants off and make yourself at home," but I knew I couldn't go through with it, so I said, "I don't feel very well. It's something I ate for supper." I wanted to get out of the room but I didn't want to offend her by not considering her attractive, so I said, "Tomorrow night," and put four dollars on the table by her bed instead of the two dollars she had mentioned in the hall, and backed away towards the door hoping I had not hurt her feelings, but all she did was to pick up the money and say, "Okay, see you later." When I got back to my room Ross said, "How did it go?" I said, "Oh, it was a terrific experience." I don't know if he believed me. Anyway, I tried.

April 22 — Saint John, New Brunswick
Here I am staying with a Miss Jack in a house full of a familiar kind of china and furniture and her talk is full of familiar names and phrases. She is a lovable old body and no mean conversationalist. She went on non-stop from supper to midnight. She has piled-up white hair, wears a black velvet band round her neck and a little watch pinned to her bosom.

April 23

This dark old house of the Jacks' smells of the yellowing newspapers stacked on every chair, but some of the furniture is beautiful and belonged originally to the Duke of Kent, Queen Victoria's father, when he was out here as Commander-in-Chief. Miss Jack provided an enormous breakfast. I ate three helpings of kedgeree. We had to conduct our conversations in whispers as Mr. Jack was still asleep. He has an all-night job as night-watchman at the city market, having fallen on lean times. However, when he did emerge he was a very distinguished-looking figure, more like an ambassador than a night-watchman. He is a jocular old gent and very much given to making puns. It must be exhausting in the long run for Miss Jack, except that as she never stops talking herself perhaps she doesn't notice. In the afternoon a youth with an enormous boil on his neck came round to take me for a walk, a task allotted to him by the Jacks. Saint John on a muggy grey Sunday afternoon is dismal. As it is built on hills one always seems to be plodding up and plodding down again. The youth, whose name was Ewing, could think of nothing better to do with me but to take me to the Saint John Park, where we gazed gloomily at some very mangy bears. When I offered him a cigarette he refused as he has some kind of crank theory that smoking is bad for the health. We went back to the Jacks' for tea. Miss Jack's married sister was there. She is more worldly than Miss Jack and knows my family. She remarked in passing in a sort of bantering fashion that they had "a somewhat exaggerated idea of their own importance".

In the evening to church in a dignified and commodious city church with comfortable pews.

April 24

In the morning went down to the theatre, or the Opera House as they call it. It is very large and excessively gloomy. The first thing that occurred to all of us was how on earth all these seats would ever be filled for our show.

To cheer ourselves, Ross and I went to the Admiral Beatty Hotel for lunch. It is a magnificent palace of a place. Ross wisely ordered the table d'hôte, which only cost ninety cents, and I foolishly ordered à la carte, which cost $2.55. This quite embittered me. Miss Jack spent the afternoon going all over town urging people to come to the play, but despite her efforts the audience was tiny and the size of the Opera House made it seem tinier still. It was most discouraging. When I got home Miss Jack was sitting up for me for a good chat which lasted on her side till my eyes were closing and I nearly fell off my chair.

April 25
In the morning I nearly missed the train. Breakfast was so leisurely as Miss Jack cannot be hurried and I was most anxious to be polite as she has been so kind. On my breakfast plate was a courtly note from Mr. Jack, who was still in bed. Miss Jack says he is quite known for the delightful notes he writes.

We arrived at St. George's in a thunderstorm. The place is a village with one straggling street. The people all turned round to stare at "the actors". We felt quite like movie stars. The whole company were seized with a fit of high spirits. It was a reaction from the fiasco at Saint John. When we were putting up the scenery we all began singing and shouting and dressing up in each other's wigs and costumes. We made such a noise that Mrs. Macrae, the chaperone, said we could be heard in the street and that people would be complaining. She is such a wet blanket. Far from complaining, the towns-people packed the hall and laughed their heads off at the play.

April 26
We are staying with the local clergyman and his wife, and I am sharing a room with Max. The clergyman is a large, ponderous, slow-moving, pipe-smoking man who

occasionally lowers a remark into the world. His wife is a pale, thin-lipped woman with a somewhat repressive manner who gave me the feeling from the first that she was not too keen to have us to stay. Max was behaving all day in a somewhat peculiar manner unlike his usual carefree self, hardly replying when spoken to. Last night when we came back after the show the truth came out. He has had a letter from his "woman" (as he always calls her although she is only eighteen) breaking off their engagement. He produced a bottle of whisky and proceeded to down one tumblerful after another, at one moment cursing her as a silly little bitch and the next moment saying that she was too good for him and that he would never amount to anything. Then he began about his boyhood, how his father used to beat him with a heavy belt with a buckle on it, how his deafness had meant that he could not keep up with the class, etc. I said, "Anyway, you are the best hockey player in college." But that did not comfort him. He said, "If I had paid more attention to studies instead of sports I might get somewhere." I said, "Perhaps you are well out of the engagement, as you say she is a bitch." He said, "I never said that. She is a swell girl, really swell, but she wants to be a goddam nurse, so she won't marry me." All this time he was pacing up and down the room, taking his clothes off as he did so and throwing them on the floor until he had nothing on. There was a rubber plant on the window-sill which Mrs. H., our hostess, had pointed out as if it was a special privilege to have it in our room. Max suddenly grabbed hold of it and shouting, "Hell's bells! What do I care?", he hurled it out of the window. I said, "That's just fine. It's going to be lovely tomorrow explaining that to Mrs. H." "All right," he said, "I will go and pick it up off the lawn," and he rushed into the hall stark naked. I went after him and said, "For Christ's sake, Max, what do you think you're doing?" but he gave me a kind of buffet on the chest, so I said, "Okay, you're right, you're just as much of a damn fool as you say you are." Then he

44

calmed down, went back into the room, and sat on the chair beside his bed and began to sob. It was pretty awful but I remembered how I had felt sometimes about Katherine, so I just swallowed down the last of the whisky and went out like a light.

April 27
When I woke up this morning the whole room was stinking of whisky, even the curtains smelt of it. I got dressed somehow, feeling pretty terrible, and went down to breakfast. There was no waking Max. He was lying like a log. Canon and Mrs. H. were sitting at the breakfast table. I plunged in right away and said, "Max and I are so terribly sorry about the accident to your beautiful plant which got knocked off the window-sill as we were undressing." Mrs. H. said, "So I observed from the remains on the lawn. One wonders how students at an Anglican college are brought up these days. It isn't only my 'beautiful plant', as you rightly call it, but the noise and the swearing. This is a Christian house, you know." Canon H. had been just sitting there puffing away at his pipe and not saying a word. Then he got up and said to Mrs. H., "You won't forget about my clean surplice for Sunday," and went out. He said nothing to me, but as he left the room he gave me a queer kind of look, not exactly a wink but nearly. Mrs. H.'s hands were trembling with suppressed rage as she took up her tea-cup. Then I had an inspiration. I said, "You know, Mrs. H., what I said just now was not the whole truth. What happened was that Max has had a disappointment in love and he was so upset that he did not know what he was doing." It worked like a charm. She looked quite softened as if she knew all about disappointments in love herself. So she said, "Poor fellow!", and that was all, which was very sporting of her, and I think I should join the diplomatic service.

45

April 28

A most unlucky day. We departed by train for Woodstock through a dull country of firs and rocks and were met by the theatre manager, a most disagreeable man with a wet cigar in his mouth. He and Hunter, our own "business manager", got into an altercation at once. The theatre manager said that practically no tickets had been sold. From what he had heard about the show, he was not at all surprised. Hunter said that if the tickets had not been sold, it was because the manager had done nothing to advertise the play. The manager said would Hunter kindly not tell him how to run his own business. Hunter said someone should have told him that long ago. Finally Hunter said, "Well, in view of your inefficiency, if it is nothing worse, we cancel our contract for the theatre." The manager said, "Not so fast, young man. Who the hell do you think you are? Just because you kids are at college you think you can get away with murder. Well, you are not going to get away with this. You owe me seventy dollars for the theatre you hired and you are going to pay it," and he walked off. This left us with the rest of the day in Woodstock as the next train doesn't leave till tomorrow morning. It was very hot and dusty and the whole company sat on the steps of the post office for hours, talking over our dilemma and then singing a few songs to pass the time. We had a lunch consisting of cold burnt potatoes and bad baked beans in a dirty feeding-place and then went to our boarding-house. Ross, Max, and I have to share one bedroom with one single bed and a cot in it. Over the bed is a photograph of a woman in black bombasine with a face like a pudding, a mean little mouth, and marbly eyes. She looks so like the proprietress of this dump that she must be her mother or grandmother. We tried to get the girls of the company to come out with us, but they were sulky and sat in a heap in the sitting-room pretending to read old magazines. Then, as we were going to bed, a police constable appeared and asked for Hunter. Mrs. Macrae, of course, lost her head and said that we would all end up in jail. The constable told Hunter that if we did not pay the seventy dollars we owed the theatre manager we would not be allowed to leave town. I don't know what authority he had to say this but Hunter, from being so arrogant in the morning, suddenly seemed quite deflated and paid over the seventy dollars.

April 29
I woke to find the whole company in a bustle of departure. We had to hurry to get the scenery on the train as, in addition to what we had paid him, the theatre manager had threatened to "impound" our scenery. We don't know if he could really do this. He seems to be able to do anything he likes in Woodstock, New Brunswick. At last we got on the train and went through some deadly dull country till we got to Fredericton. Here the streets are full of the University of New Brunswick students, who walk along in twos and threes, almost shoving you off the sidewalk. They look as if they have a pretty good opinion of themselves and have certainly not been welcoming to us, although we do come from another Maritime university. Not that we seek their company. Far from it, but it does get dull tramping the streets and not knowing anyone.

April 30
There were some letters waiting for me here, one from Anan telling me that old Mrs. Kessler was dead. She and her son, the American playwright, lived in an old crimson-brick house smelling of their innumerable cats by the lake near Port Hope, and they used to ask Peter and me to visit them from school on Sundays when we were immured at Trinity College School. They talked about plays and actors and the witty world of New York, and it was like breathing a different air from school. Mr. Kessler, the son, was a pink-faced little man with white curly hair. He wrote *Sweet Nell of Old Drury* and other musical

comedies. He made almost too much of a fuss of us, particularly of Peter. But Mrs. Kessler was the real character. Small, erect figure, pale blue eyes in a withered old face, she was interested in everything and made one feel like a human being instead of a schoolboy.

This morning after breakfast we went to the cathedral. The Dean, a pot-bellied man with a potato in his mouth, gabbled through the service and preached a nonsensical sermon. In the evening the company were all invited to his house, where we sat about for hours ranged on sofas, nibbling some special cookies made by the Dean's wife and drinking luke-warm ginger ale, and making forced conversation with some suitably churchy boys and girls who had been hand-picked to meet us. I noticed that the Dean's daughter, who was there when we arrived and was quite attractive-looking, made herself scarce early in the proceedings despite signals from her mother to remain, and I glimpsed her through the window bounding into the rumble-seat of a waiting car in company with one of the University of New Brunswick sheiks.

May 1 — Hampton, New Brunswick
This is Malcolm Dymock's home town. He is the hero of Hampton and was so riotously applauded before, during, and after the play that I could see Alice, who is acting opposite him, was looking furious as no one could hear her lines, and then he was given two bouquets and she none. One of the bouquets was brought up on stage by a wee monster of a little girl from the junior class in the school Malcolm was at here. She was bedizened with ribbons.

After the show was over Alice and I went for a walk under the stars right out of the town into some fields, and we talked and I found that, like me, she is restless and longs for fame and excitement. We wondered what it would be like to be old. Suppose I was really as old as the old man I am acting in this play, with white hair and a white moustache, hobbling about on a cane. I said to Alice that I was certain I would die young and she said she had the same premonition about herself.

I shared a room at the hotel with Max. He played his ukulele half the night. I didn't mind as I couldn't sleep anyway, but someone in the room above kept knocking on the floor. Only in the morning did we find out that the person who had been kept awake was none other than Malcolm Dymock, which was a piece of luck.

May 2 — Annapolis Royal
This place is the cradle of the race. In other words, my father's family originally came from here. The older generation, like Cousins Ella and Eliza, go on so often, too often, about the glories of The Grange, my great-grandfather's house, and the terraced gardens, orchards, broad acres, etc. I have seen a portrait of my great-grandfather. He looks a regular old curmudgeon, with little high-up eyes, like pictures of Henry the Eighth. When he was a member of the Nova Scotian Legislature, some time about 1820, he put forward a proposal to introduce negro slavery into Nova Scotia. Fortunately, hardly anyone supported the proposal. Many members of the family are buried in the old churchyard and there is a monument there to my grandfather's second wife and on it is the inscription "She did what she could". I have been in Annapolis Royal before and it always makes me feel uncomfortable. So many older people remember my family and come up to me and say, "I hope you will follow in your father's footsteps."

May 3
We crossed to Prince Edward Island. The whole train was put on the boat. Prince Edward Island seems a rich agricultural country of red earth and ploughed fields. At Souris we were met by an authoritative old lady with a wandering eye who said that as it was Sunday we must go to church, and as the only Protestant church there was a Presbyterian one, we should go to it. I have not been to

a Presbyterian church since I was a child and used to go when we stayed at Stewiacke with old Roxie. This church did not seem like a church at all. I mean to say, their service is so unmystical and undevotional.

May 4
The play was in the village hall. We had a disappointing house, which was a pity as for once we acted rather well. Most of the morning was spent patching up the scenery, which is getting very torn and tattered. We brought it all out to a meadow by the village hall and worked in the sun. I felt intensely happy, I don't know why. It just came over me. Souris consists of one long, straggling street close to the sea, which here forms a bay enclosed by red mud cliffs. Max and Alice and I went to the local café in the evening and had sundaes and started singing and keeping accompaniment by beating spoons on the table until the toothy old lady who runs the place asked us to desist. I found after the show that I had to share a bedroom with Malcolm Dymock. Actually, he wasn't too bad, almost human, except that he sleeps in his socks.

May 6 — Liverpool
All the men of the company are staying in this spacious house presided over by two exceedingly comfortable maiden ladies, one fat and rosy-cheeked, the other thin and spectacled. Liverpool is unchanged since I was here as a child ten years ago. The tree-shaded streets, the lawn-bordered houses, and the leisurely people. The place is full of corners and glimpses that bring back memories, trivial mostly, but why do these few moments survive in one's mind when the rest of that summer of 1916 has been forgotten? *Why* do I remember the fallen crab-apples in Tish Agnew's orchard, or watching the chickens' heads being cut off in the back yard of the rooming-house, or lying in bed staring at the pattern on the wallpaper one sunny morning when I woke early with Roley in the bed beside me? I can still see that wall-

paper pattern of big red roses with the sunlight shifting over them as the curtain moved in the breeze, yet I have forgotten the people and happenings of that summer almost completely. Apart from the Wainwright children with whom we played, the only person whom I remember from that time is the beautiful Mrs. Purdy. Very tall, she was in her widow's weeds. Her husband had been killed that year in the War. She used to sing in church and I watched her with adoration. The landlady at the rooming-house said once, "Mrs. Purdy has the biggest feet I have ever seen on a woman," and I hated her for the sacrilege.

May 7
The tour is over. I don't know how much money we have made for King's. Damn little, I should say. But it has been great fun. I shall miss going everywhere with the company. It gives me a feeling of reassurance and I will miss them all, even Dymock. Of course, I will see them at King's, but that will be different. After sharing so many laughs and mishaps and intimacies it will seem strange to meet them as separate people. The strangeness began today when Max and some of the girls came out here to tea. It was not a success. When I came up the drive with Max that Burgess girl was sitting on the porch steps reading a book. I introduced Max. She lifted her eyes from her book, gave him a glance, muttered "Hello", and went right on reading. I suppose she had jumped to the conclusion that he was not what Mrs. Macrae used to call "Socially okay". Who does she think she is? — vacant, empty-headed nonentity. We had tea in the library and Mother came in and was splendid, but somehow the whole thing was forced and I did not feel that they would come back. It is nobody's fault, but it is depressing.

May 10
Katherine had said that she would go to early Communion with me, so I set my alarm clock at six so as to be sure

not to be late. It was a grey, overcast day. I walked through the silent woods and over the fields to the Almons'. We had arranged that I would throw a handful of gravel from the Almons' driveway up to Katherine's bedroom window as a signal to come down in order not to wake the household by ringing the doorbell. The moment I had thrown the gravel I realized I had thrown it at Colonel Almon's window by mistake. Thank heaven he did not wake up or I should never have heard the end of it. Katherine heard the noise and put her head out, looking pretty, pink, and sleepy like a child. I thought she would never come down and that we should be late. But at last she did, wearing her broad-brimmed straw hat and carrying a pair of gloves, which I have never seen her do before. I thought we looked quite the respectable married couple going sedately to church. There were quite a lot of people we knew at the service and as I walked up the cathedral aisle with Katherine I thought, "This might be our wedding and these the wedding guests." As we knelt together at the Communion rail in the flower-scented cathedral I felt a wave of happiness come over me.

The rest of the day was anticlimactic. Gerald came to lunch as he always does on Sundays. He is mother's nephew, the son of her sister who died when he was born. His father is a retired colonel who lives in Cheltenham. Gerald must be about thirty but he seems no particular age. He never can keep any job for more than a few months and the only thing he cares about is the theatre. He acts often in amateur theatricals here. He is stout, red-faced, always seems to be sweating, and his clothes are always too big for him. I don't know why but it is so. Mother tries to look after him and to help him in any way but she gets very exasperated by him. I suppose he is a pathetic person but he is extraordinarily boring as he never stops talking about himself and the rows he has with actors and actresses in the Amateur Dramatic Society.

There was a tea party here in the afternoon, none too successful I thought, though when it was over Mother and Aunt Millie both agreed that it had been a great success, but then they always say that about our tea parties. The two Appleton-MacTavish girls were at last asked to the house, something they have been angling after for months. They are tall, angular, and flat-chested and will pretend to know people they don't know, which is silly in a small place like Halifax. They are bent on social advancement, egged on by their old mother, who got me in a corner and moaned at me till I nearly went mad. Still, there is something pathetic about them — they try so desperately hard. Really the girls at the party could have entered a competition for unattractiveness. The winner would have been the Wilmots' niece, Miss Ferguson, in her pie-crust glasses and a dress covered with buttons. However, she met her match in Cyril, who has now announced that he is going to become a clergyman. They had a lovely time together talking about the horrors of evangelism as they are both equally high church.

Went to bed early and read some of my favourite Horace Walpole letters which I keep by my bed in their limp red leather cover, and went to sleep thinking of Katherine.

May 20

Tony Fox has newly arrived from England to a job in some kind of an export firm here. I was curious to meet him. People have been talking about him and they don't know what to think of him. They say he is very sophisticated. He appeared at tea today. He was clad in the palest fawn flannels and he walked in a sauntering way into the drawing-room with his head a little on one side. He is small and slight with a pointed face, large grey eyes, and hair already receding, although he can't be more than twenty-three. He speaks in a low, soft voice. He talked to me about books and poetry. When I mentioned Rupert Brooke he said, "He has a mind like an overripe peach, don't you think?" This shocked and amused me. He has promised to lend me some novels by Aldous Huxley. He says everyone in London is reading them but that they have not penetrated here. When he left he said, "We must meet again. It is so nice to find someone civilized in this town." Of course this flattered me.

May 23

At last I am beginning to make some progress with Katherine. She came out here this evening and for once all the family were out and we were alone in this house. We rolled up the rug in the hall and danced to some of our favourite tunes on the gramophone: "Tea for Two", "No, No, Nanette", etc. Then we went into the library and I lit the fire, although it is spring now and quite warm. We talked a bit and she was more natural than usual, not being flirtatious. She told me about her family and how hard up they are and said she dreaded the idea of being really poor, that every time she walked down a street in the slums near the Citadel she thought, "Imagine if I ended up here." Then she said, "Does your mother approve of me?" and I stupidly said, "Of course she does but she does not think about you very much." She said, "I mean would she approve of our getting married or would she think that I was not good enough for you?" I said, "You don't know my mother. She is not like that at all," and she said, "I wonder." Then she said, "Well, she doesn't need to worry. I don't want to get married to you or anyone else that I have met yet. I'll probably end up an old maid." This made me laugh, as anyone less like an old maid than Katherine would be hard to imagine. After a time we stopped talking and lay side by side on the library sofa. I felt her body against mine and began kissing her. At first she kissed me back but when I began trying to undo the top of her dress she said, "No. It is nice like this. Don't spoil everything," so I stopped and we lay together, her arms around me, watching the flickering reflections of the fire. I was happy.

May 27

Tony Fox asked me to go to the movies with him. After the film there was a song-and-dance act — a chorus of girls prancing up and down, not very good, but I was quite enjoying it when I noticed that Tony was stooped over in his seat with his head in his hands and his eyes closed. I asked him if he was ill and he said no, but that the noise of the band had given him a headache, so we left. When we got out into the street I said, "The dance act was not too bad," and he said quite crossly, "How could you enjoy it? It was atrocious, blaring and vulgar." I felt I had sunk in his estimation. Then he began to talk about his impressions of Halifax and the people he had met since he came here. He was very amusing about their pretensions. He sees this place from the outside — from the London point of view — and says it reminds him of the provincial town of O in a Russian novel. On the way back we went into the Greek's in Barrington Street. It is really a small grocery store kept by a bald, ancient man with a puckered face who looks, as Tony said, like a troll in a fairy tale. There are two or three tables where you can have coffee. We sat there talking and smoking. (Tony never has a cigarette out of his mouth.) He said how much he admired my mother and that she made him think of some great actress. I said, "She is the least actressy person in the world." He said, "Yes. Perhaps it is those magnificent dark eyes with their changing expressions. You feel she understands everything and yet she could be alarming." Then he said, "I have met your inseparable friend, Peter." "What do you think of him?" I asked. "He is a charming creature, so nice to look at, but very superficial. You are much more interesting." I thought this a pretty sound verdict.

May 28

The night of Tommy Masters' twenty-first birthday party. There has never been anything to equal this in Halifax before, I mean for the younger set. In the first place the invitations said dinner jackets for the boys, which some did not have. Fortunately I had one as Mother had bought me one for the Government House ball. Some had to hire theirs. When we arrived a real butler was at the door to take our coats. He was so dignified-looking that Roddy McLaren shook hands with him thinking he was Mr. Masters. There was a silver salver in the hall with pink carnations tied with wire for the boys to put in their buttonholes. Then we all assembled, thirty-two guests in the drawing-room. The Masters have changed the room entirely from what it used to be before they bought the house from the Chamberlins. I remember it as a kid. It was a gloomy room with a round table in the middle with albums on it and old Mrs. Chamberlin, sitting by the fire, huddled up in a woollen shawl. Now it is furnished in the latest style with huge sofas and velvet "poufs" scattered about and quantities of silver-framed photographs on the top of the piano, mostly photographs of Mr. Masters receiving celebrities, including members of the Royal Family. He is away in Ottawa attending some important meeting. Mrs. Masters welcomed us in a kind of trailing purple velvet tea-gown. She said to the butler, "Have Alfred pass the cocktails," so a spotty youth appeared, only about our age, and I recognized him as he works around the gym at college. He must have been hired especially for the occasion. This was only the second time that I had had cocktails and these were very strong but they didn't make us very merry. The girls talked in lowered voices to each other. They all had new dresses for the occasion, except Katherine, who was wearing the only evening dress she has, but she looked lovelier than any of them. Tommy, although he was the host, only came in when we were all there already. He is a handsome fellow. I don't know him at all well as he is three years older than me and went to college in Ontario. He is quite jovial and I like him. Anyway, he tried to cheer the party up and downed two cocktails in quick succession. He went straight for Katherine. He has only met her twice before but he seemed to know her quite well already. I thought she seemed different from her usual self with him . . . not exactly shy but more uncertain. Finally, we all trooped in to dinner, and what a dinner: lobster and duck, and champagne flowing, finger bowls with rose petals floating in them. I sat next to a girl from Ottawa who is staying at the Masters'. She told me about the ceremony of being presented to the Governor-General, which she says is just like being presented at Court in London, and the girls wear plumes and trains. At first I thought her attractive, but then I thought she was rather boring as she hardly listened to anything I said but kept looking round the table and trying to join in other conversations.

After dinner the carpet in the drawing-room had been taken up and we danced. They had hired an orchestra. It should all have been great fun but somehow it wasn't — a sort of pall of dullness seemed to hang over the house and everyone was on their best behaviour, except Tommy, and I felt sorry for him as I could see that he knew that the party was not a real success. Towards the end he gave up all attempts at playing the host and danced only with Katherine. The Ottawa girl who had been my neighbour at dinner said to me, "Who is that girl? I hear she is some kind of a nursemaid." I said, "She comes of an old English county family." However, I can see that the other girls resent Katherine as an intruder and she has no friends among them. Silly snobs. It's because of her job. Also Fran Horsely said to me, talking of Katherine, "She is boy crazy."

May 29
Tony has lent me *Those Barren Leaves* by Aldous Huxley and I have read it through at one sitting and I am beginning to re-read it. It is different from any book I have ever read, so brilliant and witty and so modern. It makes other novels seem dated or silly. Tony came out this evening for bridge. He turns out to be a first-class bridge

57

player and must have found family bridge with us hellish, but he was very patient. He was very attentive to Mother and made her laugh by some of his descriptions of people, and I think she is beginning to like him better. At first she was far from enthusiastic. Now she thinks he is lonely in Halifax and that appeals to her sympathy. When he left, I walked down the drive with him and we continued over the railway bridge and into the park. It was a fine moonlight night and we sat on the bench overlooking the harbour mouth. The sea was perfectly calm. We talked on and on but what did we talk about? It is hard to remember, although it was only last night and we seemed at the time to be saying profound and revealing things. He has a deeply pessimistic view of the world and of himself. At the same time he is a most amusing companion with a sharp eye for all absurdities in situations and people. He is much more experienced than I am. Of course he is four years older. He has seen a lot more of the world. Some of the things that he told me about sexual practices between men and women and also between men and men were a complete revelation to me. I never could have imagined them. Tony is not happy, but he says that it is a mistake to imagine that one would be happier in another place, that if life fails it doesn't matter where you are, whereas I always think that in a new place I would be a different person and lead a new life. For instance, I imagine myself at Oxford, surrounded by troops of friends and drinking in new knowledge and new impressions. I think Peter is becoming jealous of my friendship with Tony and he takes it out by trying to make fun of him, saying he is old-maidish about his health and his eternal headaches. At the same time he is making every effort to know Tony better, and Tony, although he talks about Peter's "prattle", obviously likes him and finds him attractive.

May 30

Katherine and the children came out in the morning. It was a lovely hot day so I decided to scrap lectures and go down to the Arm with Katherine for a bathe. In the end she and I did not go in swimming. We sat on an overturned log by the wharf watching the children splashing about in the shallow water. Katherine never stopped chattering about the Masters' dinner party and about how glamorous Tommy was. She was tactless enough to say that a man of the world like Tommy was very different from boys, by whom she obviously meant Peter and myself. As she went on like this I began to feel a real hatred for her, mixed with a crashing boredom. I thought, if only I could just roll this log with you on it deep into the Arm. She didn't seem in the least aware of my feelings and for all I counted she might have been talking to the log itself. However, when we were walking home she at last noticed my stony silence and said, "Don't sulk, because I do care for you, you know." So I said, "I am not sulking; I am sad," and I turned off the road and scrambled down the side of the railway cutting, leaving her with the children.

May 31

In the evening Peter called for me in his new car and we motored down to Water Street and the harbour front. Silent stony streets, darkened shops full of ropes and nautical gear. The lights from the ships riding anchor in the harbour; drunks lurching about with eyes like dead fish; prostitutes with white powdered faces; long-limbed sailors on their way to the brothels, and also some respectable citizens heading in the same direction. I wondered if I would catch a glimpse of my cousin George with his tobacco-stained white beard on his way there. They say that when he is playing bridge at the club he suddenly jumps up in the middle of playing a hand, gets on his bicycle, and pedals down to his favourite brothel.

Peter and I saw a sign saying "fortune teller" and went

59

in. There was a gypsy-like woman there with flashing dark eyes and her head done up in a coloured scarf. The room was stinkingly dirty and two stinkingly dirty children were playing under a table. The woman led first Peter and then me behind a beaded curtain to tell us our fortunes. She told Peter he would have a life of adventure and travel over many seas. When I got in she asked me for fifty cents more than the dollar she said she charged. When I said I hadn't got it she said I was no gentleman and she could see nothing in my hand, but that I could come back later with the fifty cents.

June 1

This afternoon Grant came out in his car. He was at school with me. He is tall and red-headed and very adventurous. He has just come back from two months with a bootlegging crew out of Lunenburg and earned a lot of money. He said why didn't I go with him the next time. I should love to do this but I expect there would be opposition at home. We picked up Peter and his sister Joan and Sue Murphy and started off down the St. Margaret's Bay Road in high spirits, but while Grant was lighting Sue's cigarette the car overturned in the ditch and we were all thrown out on top of each other in a heap. We were only bruised and it was rather fun. We pushed the car back on the road and somehow it got back to Halifax, but Grant says it is damaged internally. Anyway it was only a third-hand car. When I got home I did not mention the accident to my mother as older people get into such a fuss.

June 2

The blow has fallen. I got the exam results today and I have failed again, this time not in algebra but in geometry by only two marks short of the pass mark. Better than last year when I only got fourteen out of a hundred, but I'll have to take the supplementary exams as a last hope. Mother says it is a scandal that my whole academic career and future should be held up by some pedantic nincompoop failing me by two marks, and that she is going to speak to the Minister of Education, which she is quite capable of doing. Ironically enough, the same day I got word that I had won the Welsford Prize for classics. I don't know how I did unless there were very few other competitors, as my Latin is not all that good.

Tony says that it is nonsense, my not being able to do maths, that if one has intelligence one can apply it to anything. But he does not understand that after my repeated failures maths has become to me like the porridge that I could not eat as a kid.

June 3
I have taken up fencing at the suggestion of Rodney, the Wilmots' son, who is a very nice chap studying theology at King's. The fencing takes place in the Dalhousie Gymnasium. I am improving but I shall never be a great swordsman. Fabian Rockingham was there. He is wonderfully graceful and when I watched him fencing I realized how far I was from the ideal. I wish I knew him and his friends better. They are in a set of their own at college and all have cars.

In the afternoon I went to tea with Prof. and Mrs. MacMechan. He is the Professor of English. He has a beard and pince-nez on a ribbon. He is very Victorian intellectually but he is the most inspiring lecturer. If it had not been for his lectures I would never have read Milton, that marvellous poet, and his lectures on Shakespeare have opened up a whole world to me. Somehow you would never think it of him when he is sitting there at the tea-table eating buttered muffins and complaining about modern youth while Mrs. MacMechan purrs over the tea cups.

June 4
There was a lecture this morning from Prof. Munroe about communism and intellectual élites. I should certainly be a communist if I was poor and down and out,

but I cannot understand rich communists. As for intellectual élites, they sound hell.

Tony subjects all motives to analysis, including his own motives, and the results are sometimes devastating. After listening to him I often feel that all sorts of things I have said and done spontaneously would look very differently under his microscope. Also, my ideas about life and conduct, my taste in life and people seem crude compared with his subtlety. For instance, when I talk to him of Katherine, which I cannot resist doing, he says that my love for her is not love at all but a mixture of vanity and romanticism. That I have read somewhere about a beautiful young girl and a lovelorn suitor and that I want to feel more than I do. Also about my friendship with Peter, he says that it is not real friendship but competition, and that Peter is always trying to get ahead of me and that I resent this. As he went on I said, "Then I have no true feelings at all?" He quoted Bernard Shaw to the effect that when you learn something new it always feels at first as though you had lost something. All the same I do know that I love Katherine and that Peter is my friend, or do I?

June 5
Roley has arrived back from boarding-school for the holidays. He has grown quite a lot and is in tearing spirits and full of jokes. It is nice having him here. We can say anything to each other and he catches on to everything even when it is not said. We went for an early morning ride in the park. On the way back we met the Dwyer and Elliott girls on their bicycles. They are Roley's age. They were laughing and flirting with Roley and Roley says the Elliott girl has "it". I suppose it is all right for these kids of fifteen to be so advanced but it is a bit funny at their age.

We got back to the stables and sat on the stable floor watching William talking to two Irish-Americans from Boston who were hiring horses. William was putting on the Irish charm and playing them up like anything, saying that he could see from the beginning they were real horsemen and that there were so few about now, not like the old days, and they swallowed it all and rode off feeling like squires in old Ireland.

In the evening I went into the Greek's and bought two red apples to take to Tony who is ill in bed with flu. I thought he would associate them with the evenings that we have spent talking together at the Greek's and be pleased with them and he was. Tony has the first grown-up mind that I have ever met and being with him has stimulated my mind, but I realize that he has one obsession, and that is homosexuality. He goes on and on about it, and although it is a fascinating subject one gets tired of hearing it talked about interminably.

June 7
I took Sue Murphy to the cableship dance. I went without my glasses and in my new dinner jacket and I didn't look as bad as usual. When we got there the dance was well underway. The cableship young set were whooping it up. There were coloured balloons strung up, and they turned out the lights and we had to jump up to catch the balloons. Drinks were flowing and I had a lot of rum punch — four glasses. I went on deck with the Murphy girl and we stood clasped together beside a funnel, and then climbed into a lifeboat and pulled down a tarpaulin cover and stayed there sometime until Grant came on deck with the Pringle girl and by ill fortune headed for the same lifeboat and pulled back the tarpaulin and there we were. So they backed away hastily. It could have been embarrassing but Sue said, "What does it matter as we love each other." I do wish she would leave love out of it. The minute she said that I felt like having a drink, so we went back to the dance and I had two strong whiskies and who should descend on me but Mrs. Hickman. I was surprised to see her there as she is so much older. She wore a dress covered with flowers and a long

63

train, and her red hair was piled up but seemed to be coming down. She kept on calling me "darling". She used to be an actress in New York, or she tried to be one and then came home. We danced together but not very successfully as she, like me, had had a lot to drink. She kept on dancing right through "God Save the King" and I couldn't get her to stop. The cableship officers looked as though they thought we were almost disloyal. When Sue and I went down the gang-plank we were both in high spirits, but when we got to the late-night tram and it began swaying along and jolting over the rails, I felt sweat coming on my forehead and Sue said, "How pale you look. Is there anything wrong?" I said, "Of course not," but when I got home I lay down on my bed and squinted up my eyes at the picture over the fireplace and instead of two girls and a collie dog in the picture I saw four girls and two collie dogs. Then the whole room welled up over me and I was sick in such a hurry that I didn't have time to get to the bathroom but was sick in the wastepaper basket.

I am writing this account the next day when I am still feeling very queasy. I had to tell Mother about the wastepaper basket and being sick as otherwise Georgina would have seen and smelt it when she came to do the room. Mother was very sporting and only said, "Accidents will happen. I hope you enjoyed yourself. Take the wastepaper basket and empty it into the railway cutting." I did. Unfortunately, I met Aunt Millie while I was carrying the wastepaper basket through the hall, but she didn't notice, or pretended not to.

In the afternoon I raised the question with Mother of my going with Grant to take a job on the bootlegger. Perhaps it was not the most tactful occasion to have chosen. She said, "If you are so keen to get away, Cousin Reg would get you a job in a construction camp." As she well knows that this would not appeal to me, the whole subject was dropped.

June 8

I intend from now on to be a different person, much more vigorous and enthusiastic. Instead of skulking away if I meet someone in the street who makes me feel self-conscious I shall go right up to them and start a conversation or at least say something pleasant and pass jauntily on.

Mr. Cady is staying here — Aunt Millie and Aunt Lucy's brother. He is a nice man of fifty, pleasant and unaffected, and has a business out west. He is fat, placid, good-natured, and contented with his lot. Aunt Lucy looked beautiful today in a lilac dress and I can see how anyone could be in love with her although she's over forty. In the evening quite a lot of people came out here including Susan Carpenter on a visit from England. We used to play croquet together when we were children and I was staying with her family in Dorset and she always cheated. She now wears glasses, has a stye in her eye, and a face like a tightly drawn hospital window-blind. We sat about in the library, smoking cigarettes and discussing various things including rattlesnakes and modern drama.

June 11

The Almons have a relation called David Martineau from England staying with them. Colonel Almon says that he is a rolling stone and has had all sorts of jobs all over the world but can never settle down to any of them. Now he has bought a fruit farm in British Columbia and is going out there to live. (Why do all these Englishmen, like Katherine's father and so many others, think that they can make a success of fruit farms, which almost always seem to fail?) He is quite old — at least forty but looks much younger, quite like a young man until you get right up to him. He has fair hair and a fair moustache. He seems nice and modest but I think he has his eye on Katherine. She seems rather to like him. I don't mean that she is in love with him but I think she confides in him. Colonel Almon says that they sit up together until all hours talking. I don't quite know what to make of

65

him. He has some strange ideas; for instance, he told me the other day that he was convinced that our Lord would come back to earth on a certain date next year and that this would be Judgment Day and the end of the world. I can't see why if he believes this he bothers to start a fruit farm.

Aunt Millie says that everyone in town is talking about Katherine and Tommy Masters as they are inseparable, and that she is being very silly and that Katherine has lost her head about him.

I was very depressed about this. Aunt Lucy saw it and she was very sweet. We danced to the gramophone in the hall and had quite an intimate chat. She was most understanding but can you trust older people? They draw you out and then talk you over among themselves. I don't really think Aunt Lucy is like that. She told me tonight that Mr. Cady is an atheist. I was astounded — I didn't think he had it in him.

I went to my bedroom early in a mood of defiance and read *Henry Fox's Diary* instead of working at mathematics for the supplementary exam next month. I like a diary better than memoirs; it is less made up afterwards to favour the writer. I was pleased that Sidney Smith, the clergyman wit of the Holland House circle, said, "I prefer breakfast to any other meal: people do not boast at breakfast."

June 13

I played golf with Mr. Cady in the morning. I cannot afford a proper set of golf clubs, which makes my golf very erratic as my driver is no good and I usually have to drive with an iron. The Gorsebrook course is not really professional as boys are playing football on it.

June 15

Tony Fox has written Peter what amounts to a love letter. Peter showed it to me today and treats it as a great joke. I feel sorry for Tony if he is in love with Peter and think him very silly to have written this letter which Peter will show to everybody.

Peter took me for a drive to Waverley today. He is in the highest of spirits as he is off to England this month to spend the summer before going to Cambridge in the autumn and is full of fantastic plans for the future. He makes nothing seem impossible or impractical. That is one reason why I am so fond of him. To so many people everything seems impossible except to go on in the same old way from day to day. In some ways Peter is quite like a schoolboy still, I mean we begin laughing and singing and fooling about and it is fun. I know that Tony is far cleverer and more sophisticated than we are, but then he is older and subjects everything to analysis, whereas Peter does not know what analysis means and enjoys adventure and misadventure; in fact he prefers the latter. He positively enjoys it when his car breaks down, which it does almost every day. I shall miss him when he goes.

June 28

Woke up early and read some of *Plato Book II*. What a revelation it is. What a pity the classics professor Murray is such a whiskered old lobster and so pedantic.

Went to an evening party at the Murphys', Sue's parents. They seem nice enough people, but Mrs. Murphy is an Upper Canadian and is always referring to high society in Toronto. Also there is a brother called Michael with a long nose, and very nosy too, as the moment Sue and I got alone together and were petting on the sofa, he had to come in on the pretence that he was looking for some gramophone needles. After that we went back to the drawing-room and did some table turning, which was excessively boring as no spirits came and I don't wonder — I would not have gone to that party if I had been a spirit. Then Peter, who was there, told some ghost stories, the same old ones, but they fell flat.

June 29

Got up in a very bad temper and felt like throwing my bacon and eggs at someone's head. Instead, I set out along the railway cutting to fence with Rodney Wilmot.

In the evening Tony came out and Mary Binney and Captain Shaw, who is here in the Army, and we did table turning and then blindfolded Mary Binney and willed her to touch some object in the room on which we were all concentrating, in this case the clock on the mantelpiece. She did identify it, but it does not prove anything as Mother would give hints. Later in the evening Professor Walker telephoned with great news: If I can pass my math supplementary I can qualify for "Junior Colonial Status", which means entrance to Oxford. He thinks that Pembroke College will accept me. It is said to be a small but attractive college. Its great attraction for me is that it has no college entrance exam.

July 1

Tony and I went to the movies tonight — *The Dancer of Paris* with Dorothy MacCail. She is beautiful, but the picture had been so much censored that it was difficult to follow. Afterwards we came back to his rooms and he gave me two whisky and sodas which made me feel rather sick but I didn't show it.

Mrs. Bright, our old cook, died today in hospital. She was with us when I was a child. Her husband used to be the coachman. I remember once when there was a thunderstorm and lightning flashed, Mother saw Mrs. Bright walking up and down in the kitchen in her flannel nightgown looking, she said, like "Noah's wife". Mother asked why she did not go back to bed. She said, "I can't sleep for knowing that Bright is burning in hell." Mother said, "How can you say that, Mrs. Bright? He was such a good man." "No," she said, "Bright is burning. He took the Lord's name in vain every day of his life."

July 3

An unlucky day. There was no water. Some nonsense about the rates not being paid. Mrs. Eccles, a great friend of Mother's who is staying here, had a sort of fit at breakfast, so the rest of us withdrew to the kitchen and had breakfast there, not to embarrass her. William is drunk again. I walked up through the railway cutting for fencing and did so badly that even Rodney is thoroughly discouraged.

In the afternoon I went for a ride. A very stupid horse constantly trying to crop grass by the roadside, a struggle to keep her moving at all. What strong necks horses have. It was very hot and the horse and I were sweating profusely, so that all in all the ride was more a duty than a pleasure.

I have not seen Katherine for nearly two weeks but I met her walking up from the tram today. She now treats me as though I were a schoolboy and, worse still, she has taken to confiding in me her passion for Tommy, who is a resplendent figure in her eyes, rich and grown-up and a man of the world. The strange thing is that I am not as jealous of Tommy as I was of Peter and Bill and the other boys. I realize that I could not possibly compete with him.

July 4

Mary Binney came to tea. In conversation she always tends to agree with the strongest. It is partly because she is so very hard up. She has to wear clothes given her by other people, but she is never dispirited. Some people say she is a "hunger marcher", always out for a free meal. She and her mother, old Mrs. Binney, only have $500 a year to live on. Mary is not young but she seems ageless. Today she brought with her some English friends, Colonel and Mrs. du Plat Taylor. He is a retired colonel, with the most ill-fitting set of false teeth. He is quite overshadowed by Mrs. du Plat Taylor, an imposing lady of aristocratic antecedents, with smooth chestnut hair parted in

69

the middle and protuberant blue eyes. She looks like a face in a portrait by a Victorian painter. Their daughter, Cynthia, is an out-of-door girl, quite hard to talk to but sincere. The du Plat Taylors have bought a farm in Newfoundland and are going to settle there and begin a new life. Mrs. du Plat Taylor's cousin, Captain Campbell, whom I met last year, was an explorer and went with Captain Scott to the Pole.

July 5
The du Plat Taylors have asked me to go to work on their farm in Newfoundland. Mary Binney is going there to stay with them and we will go together. I am very keen on this plan, although it will be hard work and I have never done any farm work before. I talked it over with Mother and she agrees, so I am going to take carpentry lessons so that I can help around the place.

July 6
In the afternoon my first carpentry lesson in preparation for Newfoundland from a splendid old Scotchman with a long white beard. He is the soul of honour and intelligent and he told me that his father reviewed German philosophical works and wrote historical books. The actual carpentry is not so interesting and the awl is hard to learn how to handle.

July 7
Another carpentry lesson. I do not seem to be making much progress and the carpenter, although a fine man, is really very boring and told me all over again about his father's reviewing the book on German philosophy.

July 9
What news! I have passed the geometry supplement exam and "quite creditably" but I can hardly believe it. I bought two new books today, one I have begun reading: *The Dance of Life* by Havelock Ellis, difficult but absorbing.

I have to make a Latin oration on receiving the Welsford Prize. Old Mr. Logan, who used to be a Latin teacher, has been persuaded by Mother to help me (in fact, write it for me). When my mother decides to fascinate someone she seldom fails. Mr. Logan sat on the sofa in the library with his eyes popping out while Mother showed more interest in him than anyone has for a long time. Still, he is a good old sort.

July 12

I walked up to King's through the woods and climbed the rough stone walls between our woods and Gorsebrook woods and I felt a kind of rush of love for Nova Scotia, for these woods and this place where I was born. I thought of the games we used to play in these woods when we were kids and we pretended that the stream was the St. Lawrence River and Roley and I and the three Wainwrights divided into two camps: English against French. I was the French commander Montcalm and built a stone fort by the stream by pulling loose stones out of the walls between the woods. It was supposed to be the Citadel of Quebec and we enacted the battle of the Plains of Abraham. One time we would let the English win and the next time, the French. As Montcalm, I died a hero's death pierced by my wounds. The remains of the fort are still there and now the Almon children play in the woods.

There was an informal meeting at King's to organize ordeals for the freshmen when they arrive next September. Anderson, that petty boss, was presiding, immensely self-important, so was Cyril. The damn fools — they want to order that the freshettes must carry open umbrellas, rain or shine, for three weeks when they first arrive.

July 13

The day started badly with a long discussion of our finances. Mother says we are on the brink of ruin, yet she knows how much I want to go to Oxford next year and

71

has been trying to raise the money. Apart from the fees, I would have to have an allowance of at least £300 a year and Roley still has to be kept at Trinity College School and there is the cost of bringing him to and from Ontario for the holidays, and the up-keep of this place. The vine is smothering the front of the house and should be cut down, and the drive is in a terrible condition of holes and bumps and needs to be re-gravelled. Then, of course, there is the fact that there are always people staying here or coming for meals and mother regularly helps some people who are hard up financially, particularly her nephew, Gerald.

Then I walked into town and bought some flowers for Katherine as it is her birthday, but the only ones I could afford were some mingy carnations. I called in on the Carsons on the way home. There they were, the whole family, seated on their separate perches in the sitting room like a lot of silly, grave penguins.

An evening at home. Mother read aloud *The Call of the Wild* by Jack London. A fascinating book. I like these evenings in the library with the curtains drawn and my mother's voice reading. When the others had gone to bed I lay on the sofa and fell half asleep and thought that perhaps some day I would look back to this room and these evenings when I was old.

July 14
I worked all morning on my thesis on *Comus*. A good many phrases are cribbed. I wonder if Professor MacMechan will spot them. I don't put it past him.

There is an English theatrical company in town, the Glossop-Harris Company, presided over by Miss Glossop-Harris, who looks, or tries to look, like Reynolds' portrait of Mrs. Siddons. They are a splendid company. Tony and I went to the *School for Scandal*. It is a long play but so well acted, and Sheridan's wit has kept most of its tang. Afterwards Tony and I went to the Greek's for coffee and then walked round and round Citadel Hill, talking.

72

July 15

Major Uniacke came out to breakfast in the library with Aunt Lucy presiding. The two of them are going to Mount Uniacke tomorrow for a long stay. Aunt Lucy loves Mount Uniacke, where she spent so much of her girlhood, and she looked beautiful this morning, so pleased to be going there. She is a darling, sweet without being insipid.

In the evening we all went to see *Macbeth*: Mother, Aunt Millie, Aunt Lucy, Gerald, Eileen, Peter, and me. We had a box, a great extravagance, and it meant that we could hardly see a thing on the stage except by taking turns to crane over the edge of the box from the three chairs in the front of it. *Macbeth* is the greatest play in the world; I think I enjoyed it more reading it than seeing it acted. Miss Glossop-Harris as Lady Macbeth seemed quite to overwhelm Macbeth, who just seemed henpecked. Incidentally, somebody told me that Miss Glossop-Harris is quite enamoured of the actor who played Macbeth although he is twenty years younger than she is.

July 16

Honey and rolls for breakfast. I ate at least nine rolls. I read all morning for my government course about socialism and individualism. I am disgusted to discover that I am a late-Victorian individualist. I don't know which I dislike more, a meddling imperialist state or a meddling socialist state. Why can't they leave us alone?

In the evening I went with Eileen to *Romeo and Juliet,* acted by the Glossop-Harris Company. It bowled me over so completely and the poignancy of the parting scene was so unbearable that tears were running down my face. Thank goodness Miss Glossop-Harris herself decided not to play Juliet, although she toyed with the idea. Eileen and I came back in the tram together and then walked the rest of the way home. She talked to me as she used to do when we were younger, and I saw that though she hides it she is very restless and not too happy. She has

73

nothing to do, and talks of the possibility of getting a job. Dear Eileen, how fond I am of her and always will be.

She does not like Tony at all, in fact disapproves of him. I cannot understand people disapproving of others; I thought only the old did that.

Peter sails for England day after tomorrow. Mother had a large tea-party of women. I heard much clattering of tea-cups so I escaped and dropped in at Peter's, but he was out and I was left all alone with old Mrs. Archibald. She was in a very amiable mood and gave me a copy of a poem she has written in praise of ether (how it prevents pain, etc.). I thought it was very imaginative. She certainly is pleased with it herself. Her son and his wife and their daughter came in later. These are the relations who Peter says have supplanted him in Mrs. Archibald's favour. I had expected to see some sinister schemers but they appear to be perfectly nice, ordinary people.

In the evening Roley and I went to the Strand Theatre with Gerald. It was a bit hectic like every time one appears in public with Gerald. He looked so peculiar that everyone was staring at us. He kept his tweed cap on throughout the performance and pushed it on the back of his head and his overcoat was much too big for him, yet he asked the woman in front of us in a very hoity-toity voice, "Please remove your hat as others in the audience have an equal right to see the performance." She gave him a very dirty look but unpinned her hat and put it in her lap. Then some people pushed past us to take the seats next and Gerald said if anyone else interrupted us he would punch them in the nose. Poor Gerald, as if he could punch anyone in the nose or anywhere else, and he talked so loudly in his English voice. He was not drunk but I think he is more than a little mad. Two King's students were sitting behind us, one of them Fabian Rockingham, whom I particularly admire — at a distance. I could hear them laughing at us. I suppose going about with Gerald is good for Roley and me. We can never be self-conscious in public later on after this training.

The show was a vaudeville, absolutely putrid — a Spanish dance with a lot of clacking castanets, danced by quite an elderly female who looked somewhat like Mary Binney, and afterwards a sickening minuet. When I got home I described Gerald's behaviour to Mother and said how awkward it made me feel, and all she said was, "Gerald may be a little peculiar but he is your cousin, and blood is thicker than water. I should not have thought you were so feeble as to care what other people think."

July 18
Today Peter sailed for England. I went down to the boat to see him off. There were free drinks going and a crowd of people from Halifax on board going to England, mostly the smart Americanized kind of people: girls going to finishing schools in France, and mothers in elaborate dresses, and fathers red in the face from cocktails. I always feel ill at ease with these people; they seem so rich and assured, but I think that their assurance is misplaced. Peter was so surrounded with Archibalds that I could hardly talk to him, so I walked all over the boat, up and down the stairways, into the smoking-room, and inspected some cabins full of farewell flowers, and saw people lining up at the purser's office to reserve their tables in the dining-saloon, and I walked on the upper deck which smelled of white paint. Sailors were swabbing down the boards. I wished I was going on the boat to England or to anywhere. Then I forced myself to go back to the saloon where the company was gathered and to talk to Mrs. M. She had huge rings on her veined hands and said she knew Mother and Aunt Millie, which is not true, as when she spoke to Aunt Millie the other day on the tram Aunt Millie just fixed her eyes on space as if she saw something in the distance and said to me afterwards that "she drew the line" at Mrs. M. Just as the funnel was hooting to signal that the visitors must get off Peter managed to get away from the clutch of Archibalds and

75

came over to me. He looked somewhat distraught and said something about how much he was going to miss me and that it would not be long before I was over at Oxford and we would meet, but we both know that it will not be the same. As I stood on the pier watching the water between the pier and the boat widening as she drew out, I felt: this is the end of something — stopping loving Katherine and Peter going away. I walked home feeling more and more depressed and passed Tony's lodging, but I could not face his analysis or his wit. When I turned into our gates I thought of William and went down to the stables and helped him polish the harness and felt a bit better.

In the evening Mother read Proverbs and Ecclesiastes. To bed early, but I could not sleep on account of sex.

July 19

The morning was grey and sticky and I felt the weight of inertia and depression. I was rather rude to Eileen at breakfast and then went in to Miss Stewart's. She is trying to explain logarithms to me. None of my experience of mathematics, painful as it has been, has prepared me for the pure horror of logarithms, and I think poor Miss Stewart is almost as puzzled by them as I am. Walking home I determined to stop pulling a long face and I dropped in to tea at the Almons'. It was a big tea-party for the Glossop-Harris Theatrical Company. Katherine, in a black velvet dress which made her white skin seem even whiter and outlined her breasts, was enjoying the admiration of young Jarmin, the actor, who had never met her before, and sat on a footstool saying melodramatically that he would like to look at her forever. It was a gay and pleasant party but for some reason I felt rather at a loss, and I have often enjoyed myself more at duller parties where I could shine, relatively. In the evening I took Janet MacDonald to see Marie Prevost at the movies. She is becoming my favourite actress. She is so piquant. Janet is a wonderful girl, just the kind of girl I would like to be in love with if I could choose. She has splendid eyes and a straight, sincere look. We went afterwards for ice-cream sundaes to the Green Lantern. Tony came in and joined us and Janet got bored and set fire to a bowl full of matches. I liked her so much for doing this.

I came home and read Conrad's *Lord Jim*. I am possessed by the character of Lord Jim and all day I pretended that I was him, an infinitely interesting, essentially decent character. I am always pretending to be characters in books I am reading or heroes in movies, although I know it is childish.

July 20

I was reading from Herbert Spencer on "Over-legislation", a musty old volume but extraordinarily interesting. Then I looked out of the window to see the lawn and the field by the woods ablaze. We all rushed out: Georgina, William from the stables came running up, Aunt Millie and Mother and I, pounding down the flames with tin cans. It took nearly an hour and the fire was quite near the house but we finally got it out. Mother had tried to burn off the old grass without asking anyone's help. She did exactly the same thing last year and there was a fire then too, and she swore she would never do it again but she says she simply could not resist. In the afternoon Cousin Reg came out to discuss our finances with Mother. She's trying to raise extra money. It sounded from the hall to be another very heated discussion between them and she went up to her bedroom, muttering between her teeth. I joined Reg in the library and for some idiotic reason I started a discussion on the subject of eternity and the after life and asked him whether he believed in it. He seemed quite at a loss and went on humming and hawing till we dropped the subject.

Then I went up to my room and drew up a new plan for the rest of the summer: four hours' serious reading a day, no novels, exercise an hour a day, no movies, strict economy, no sundaes at the Green Lantern, walk into town instead of taking the tram, do not telephone Katherine unless she telephones me first, put a stop to sensual thoughts and actions which lead nowhere, and concentrate on acquiring knowledge, enjoying scenery, etc.

July 23
A day passed in accordance with the new plan. Read *Maines Ancient Law* and wrote notes on what I had read, then walked up and down my bedroom summarizing the notes aloud as though I were lecturing. It is a good way of driving home the points to one's self. Aunt Millie overheard me and thought I was just talking to myself and that I had gone slightly mad. In the afternoon I forced myself to go for a ride. It was a blazingly hot day. These horses are true livery-stable horses; they turn round and head for home at the end of the time that has been paid for. William started talking about his boyhood in Ireland, how his father had been a "strong farmer" but the property was divided. He had been walking out with a girl for four years but there was not enough money for the marriage on her side, so she has never married and neither has William. He says that he is not sorry when he sees the married men he knows and that his brother's wife has "a lookless look". His brother used to run the cab stand here but now he has moved into taxis. He comes to the stables often and helps William with money. Talking of my mother, William said it was a thousand pities that she had given up riding; that as a young woman she had a natural way with a horse and it was a pleasure to see her going over jumps, and that although my father loved riding, it did not come naturally to him. When I got home I found everyone was out except Mother and me. We had tea in the library. It is so seldom that we are alone together in this household so full of people. We discussed all sorts of subjects, including sex. She said she knew nothing about the physical part of marriage when she married my father, and she asked

78

Aunt Lucy, who was married already, and all she said was, "My dear, it is no worse than having your ears pierced for earrings." To me this sums up the Edwardian attitude to the subject. Her own attitude is very contradictory — on the surface she is very proper, but secretly I think she would find me an awful muff if I had no real love affairs. She talked a lot about her beloved brother Charlie and his adventures with women. I wish I could be more like him — dashing and irresistible. Then suddenly Mother was inspired to do a series of imitations of people: Cousin Reg, Gerald, Mary Binney, and Queen Victoria, whom she had seen as a girl at the Diamond Jubilee. There never was such a mimic. For days she doesn't do it at all and then it comes over her like a sneezing fit.

July 24

On my way into town today I saw Fabian Rockingham strolling along Barrington Street looking very debonair. I thought how much I wished I knew him better. I see him at fencing but only in a very casual way. When I got home I mentioned this to Mother and she said, "Why don't you just pick up the telephone and ring him up and ask him to go to a movie with you or something. Don't just sit about saying, 'I wish I knew him better,' " I hesitated because he is in a much more dashing set at college than I — in fact, I am in no set at all. However, I thought, "I'll try," so I did telephone him, trying to sound as if it was the most natural thing in the world, but it turned out just as I had thought it would: that he was going out every night next week and that he would see me at fencing sometime. Although he was perfectly polite, I felt hot with embarrassment at having rung him up like this when I scarcely know him and he obviously has no wish to know me.

Then I went for a walk by myself in the park. It seems that everything I do is wrong. I am no help to Mother in her responsibilities; I am regarded as a freak by Fabian and his crowd; I am wasting such brains as I have on trivialities; and I cannot change myself however hard I try. As I was slouching along one of the paths in the park in this state of gloom, who should I see coming towards me but the unmistakable figure of Gerald. I think he saw me first as he put on a very jaunty air and started whistling unconcernedly and then gave a start of surprise at meeting me, just as if he was putting on one of his acts at the theatre. So we walked along together. He was wearing an enormous new grey fedora hat that came over his ears and he started on one of his interminable rigmaroles, this time about his plan to go to New York, where he thinks his theatrical talents will be recognized, and away from Halifax, where no one knows anything about acting or appreciates him. Every time we passed anyone in the park Gerald would take off his hat to them and say "Good day" in a condescending manner as if they were his tenants. I said, "Do you know all these people, Gerald?" and he said, "Many people know me who I do not know."

July 26
We all went to church and the Archbishop preached on the text "Thy sin shall find thee out". I kept thinking: Yes, but will other people find out? Gerald came to lunch, as he does every Sunday. I saw him come sweating up the drive. He is always so hot, summer and winter. My heart sank when I heard his voice hallooing in the hall. Lunch was interminable. Gerald is such a slow eater and talks and talks about his amateur theatricals, whereas Mother bolts her food. Finally she said, "For the Lord's sake, Gerald, eat up. We don't want to stay here all day."

July 27
Left in the morning for Newfoundland. When I got to the station Mary Binney was waiting for me there. I couldn't help thinking how peculiarly dressed she was. She had on

a very short skirt covered with flowers that looked as if it belonged to a girl, and she is Mother's age. On her head she had a toque-style hat which seemed to be very high on her head instead of low, as toques usually are. Just as we were climbing on to the train there was a gust of wind and her hat blew off and went rocketing down the platform. I ran after it to pick it up and as I did so a lot of tissue paper blew out of the hat. Mary explained that it was a hat that had been given to her and had belonged to someone who has a bigger head than Mary, so she had to stuff it with paper. Now that the paper had blown away she just plumped the hat back on her head where it came down nearly to her shoulders, but she didn't seem to care. All the way to Sydney she talked to the other passengers, asking them all sorts of questions in her loud, confident voice and soon had the interest squeezed out of them. She is just the same with everyone and talked to the train conductor the same way she does to one of her favourite admirals.

The train was loaded on to a ferry to cross the Straits of Canso to Cape Breton and Mary and I stood on the prow smoking cigarettes. She says she smokes sixty cigarettes a day, more even than Mother.

When we reached Cape Breton the train passed by the Bras d'Or Lakes, very romantic stretches of glistening water splashed with dark-green islands and ringed about with hills of dim blue. It was like a setting for Scott's *Lady of the Lake*. From this scene the train rushed into the grimy greyness of the coal-mining country where the miners have been on strike: hard, rocky land, and little cabins where the miners live. There were men in the streets with blackened faces, sitting on their haunches staring into space, and skinny women at the doors of the houses.

At Sydney we boarded the boat for Port-aux-Basques, Newfoundland. It was a smelly little tub. I sat up quite late with Mary in the smoking saloon. She had picked up a kind American and was drinking whisky and sodas

81

with him. As we got out to sea the boat began rolling and I began to feel seasick. They said, "A whisky will settle you." I had one, but as I am not very used to whisky, it did not settle me but only made me feel sicker, so I went to my cabin, which I shared with two good-natured men who did not seem to mind my being sick in the basin. When I did get to bed, what should I see crawling over my pillow but an army of bedbugs! So I dressed and lurched upstairs to the saloon and slept on the floor next to Mary, who was sleeping peacefully on a sofa with her coat over her. For economy's sake she had not taken a cabin.

July 28

It was pouring rain and very cold in the morning. Port-aux-Basques is nothing but a fishing village, so we took the train for our destination, Black Duck. The train is very high off the ground and has old-fashioned straw seats, and it goes so slowly that they say people have walked beside it and got there first. The country is oppressive, mile after mile of marshy, barren lands, stunted trees, and little huts like animal pens where people live, all of this under a dull grey sky. At mid-day we came to Black Duck, which turned out not to be a place at all, just a train stop and a shed. Colonel du Plat Taylor and Cynthia and an enormous Newfoundland dog met us and we walked about three miles, carrying our suitcases, over a track through the woods to their house, which has just been finished. It is built of logs and has a big central room with a long wooden table. Passages lead off to the bedrooms, but I am not to sleep in one but in a tent near the house. The property adjoins that of Captain Campbell, the explorer, and du Plat Taylor's cousin. His house has plumbing; the du Plat Taylors' has not. The woods are very thick and close round the du Plat Taylors' house. It is very airless, muggy weather and the blackflies are everywhere, they even got into my tent last night. I started smoking to discourage them and burnt a hole with my cigarette in the tent. This is a bad start to my visit here as Colonel du Plat Taylor is particularly proud of his tent. It was hot during the night and I began to wonder why I had come here at all.

July 29

First day at Black Duck. It was a topping day and I know I shall enjoy myself here. There is a Captain Smith staying here. He is in the Guards, a most charming chap — tall, handsome, and awfully amusing. He took me on an exploring expedition with him today, punting upstream on the river which is on the edge of the du Plat Taylors' property. It is a fast-running salmon stream with plenty of rapids. We built a fire and lunched on Oxo and biscuits and started inland, blazing a trail with axes through the woods. The trees are dead-looking and are coated with dank moss. We came out of the woods into a great stretch of swampy ground, which they call here "mish". When you walk on it it is like walking on a sponge. There were curious scarlet flowers everywhere. I don't know what they are called. The sky was grey and the air oppressive and the stunted trees and those queer flowers and the stillness of the woods seemed somehow prehistoric. We got back to the stream very hot and stripped and swam in a pool. Captain Smith when stripped might pose for a Greek statue.

We reached home late for supper. All the food here is tinned except the fish caught in the stream. Even the milk is milk powder out of a tin. Of course, there are no deliveries here and no cows in the neighbourhood, not even in the nearest village. This doesn't worry the du Plat Taylors; in fact they enjoy discomfort and privations. Mrs. du Plat Taylor is particularly spartan and rather alarming in her contempt for what she calls "muffishness", by which she means any kind of softness. Colonel du Plat Taylor is a great advocate of common sense, which is his standard of judging people. I hope I can rise to it. Cynthia is a dear, so genuine. All the family have been kind in welcoming me and I hope I can be of some use here. Captain Smith is not a devotee of discomfort.

July 30

The first full day's work for me. Colonel du Plat Taylor took me out to the farther clearing, explained to me about sowing the grass seed, and I was left in charge of two local men to show them the work. I don't think I made any blunders. The men are from around here and are half French. I talked a lot with them. They are very entertaining company but the work went rather slowly.

In the afternoon Cynthia and I worked on making a bench. This is where my carpentry lessons should come in useful as I had the planing of the wood. Cynthia is becoming quite a friend. She is a good sort. She certainly doesn't try to be fascinating. I think her parents are rather too much for her.

I don't know how much Mary Binney is enjoying herself here. She says she has had indigestion from the food ever since she arrived. Mrs. du Plat Taylor is rather stern with her and said to me, "Why does she dress in clothes so much too young for her and such unsuitable shoes for the country?" Of course I could not tell her that Mary wears what is given her. Mrs. du Plat Taylor said, "She is mutton dressed as lamb." In the evening Mr. B. came to supper. He is an Englishman, a "remittance man": his family in England pay him a certain amount each month to stay away. He lives in a dishevelled house near here with a local girl whom he may have married. He is good company, talks a lot and drinks a lot. He has a bald head on top, curly ringlets about his ears, flashing dark eyes, and looks like a pirate. He has been all over the world and is a wanderer. He and Captain Smith had several drinks down by the stream before supper, as drink doesn't exactly flow at the du Plat Taylors'. After supper everyone was sleepy and argumentative. Captain Smith and Mr. B. are more modern in their ideas than the du Plat

Taylors, who are quite feudal in their outlook. Certain subjects irritate them into a state of violent disapproval, such as Lloyd George (because of his taxes, which have ruined the du Plat Taylors and made Mrs. du Plat Taylor give up her home on the Scottish border, where her family have lived since the twelfth century). They also disapprove of all Americans and everything American. Mr. B. unwisely said that he thought the Americans a great people. I thought Colonel du Plat Taylor's false teeth would fall right out with rage. Mary tried to pour oil on troubled waters but got snubbed for her pains.

July 31
Spent the morning overseeing the men who are sowing grass seed. The Newfoundlanders are like no other people. They have an uproarious sense of humour and independence and their poverty does not seem to quench their enjoyment of life. Captain Smith and Colonel du Plat Taylor set off today for Port-aux-Basques to buy supplies, Captain Smith clad in grey tweeds with a marvellously cut double waistcoat and a pale grey hat. I should like some day to have clothes like his. Even his roughest things are of the best. Colonel du Plat Taylor is quite a contrast, wearing an old broad-brimmed hat that all the family use at different times, with a mosquito net draped over it.

In the afternoon I cleared a lot of undergrowth, hacking away at alder bushes which are surprisingly strong and apt to spring back at you like india-rubber. Later, Cynthia and I went salmon fishing but got nothing. The flies were swarming. Never have I seen or imagined anything like the flies in this place, every variety of them. I looked down at my hand today while fishing. It was absolutely black, covered with thousands of tiny blackflies, and there are swarms of mosquitoes always round one's head, and worst of all are what they call "caribou flies". They take a real piece of meat out of one's neck and fly away with it. Of course we squirt ourselves and plaster ourselves with anti-mosquito stuff, which I think the flies find rather tasty.

August 1
Spent the morning shovelling some manure and then cut down tress, dragging up roots, etc. I am getting a bit handier with an axe but it rather worries me that I don't believe Colonel du Plat Taylor thinks I am as useful about the place as he had hoped. Probably he expected me to be a Canadian woodsman, and that I am not. He never says anything critical about my work but looks at the results silently and sighs, which makes me nervous. I do try hard.

In the afternoon Captain Campbell came over from his place and asked me to go along with him to find a lake which he had heard of from the local people but which is not on the map. It was rather a lark for me to be exploring with a man who was on Scott's expedition to the Pole. We went through an impenetrable jungle of trees and alder bushes, blazing our way on the trees with our axes, and came to a huge marsh or swamp. We climbed a hill and there we saw the lake and sat down on an up-turned tree trunk to look at it. It was a little grey lake with a lot of firs around it.

When we got back the du Plat Taylors gave us each a glass of vermouth, which I have never tasted before. Then we discussed what we should call the lake and I said, "Why not Lake Mary?", as I wanted to cheer Mary up. She has not been her usual self since we got here, very subdued. At first Mrs. du Plat Taylor was rather cool to the idea and wondered, "Why Lake Mary?", but the others all welcomed it and the name will be sent to the map-making authorities and Mary will be immortalized. Part of the trouble is that Mary does not work. Mrs. du Plat Taylor never stops planting and hoeing and making her garden and stalking about the place overseeing everything and everybody. I don't know what Mary does all day except write letters.

August 8

In the morning our party started out in the streaming rain in an open motor-boat to explore the coast. We disembarked at Stephenville to collect letters and newspapers and there the thunderstorm began. The encircling hills threw back the shock of it. The rain came down on the water, prickling the silky surface till the sea was like a pin-cushion full of little holes. In the afternoon it cleared. Cynthia and I took the ferry to Sand Point. It is a curious little village built on a spit of sand jutting into the sea. The streets of the village are sand paths with picket fences on either side and baaing sheep go strolling along the streets. On either side of the village the Atlantic pounds on a pebbly shore. There is a white wooden church and the churchyard is full of purple and yellow flowers. The wharves and the fishermen's huts face the bay.

When we came back to Stephenville the whole du Plat Taylor family took the train to Black Duck. Eric Smith and I were left with the motor-boat. We could not get away in it as the wind changed and the seas were heavy, so we put up for the night in the small hotel at Stephenville and sat talking for hours in the hotel parlour. He talked about women, of whom he has many in his life. He thinks of marrying a particularly rich one called Iris. He says she is "rather unwieldy" but quite clever. Then he talked about his Sandhurst training, how tough it was, and he lolled in a rocking-chair in his blue shirt singing obscene songs of his Sandhurst days. He said that I should go into the diplomatic service and he would wield his influence with his cousin in the Foreign Office. He has many schemes for his own future but they change every time he talks of them. He let me smoke his pipe, which made me very sick afterwards.

August 9

Back at Black Duck. Spent the morning transplanting beets and "singling" turnips. You squat down in front of a row of turnips, pull six turnips out of the row and leave the seventh, and so on and on, so that they will have a better chance to grow. It is a monotonous job, and the flies are fierce. Working with me is a man from the Hebrides whom the du Plat Taylors have imported. He is deaf and dumb and I pass the time by telling him all the secrets of my soul and body as they are safe with him. I can't help thinking that this new job of mine shows that singling turnips is about all Colonel du Plat Taylor thinks I am capable of.

In the afternoon we went fishing but caught nothing. Colonel du Plat Taylor says a local man is netting the pool and that is why the fishing isn't better. This naturally annoys him very much but he can't prove it.

Raspberry pie for supper. Boxes of the du Plat Taylors' books arrived from England. Mrs. du Plat Taylor got out the Baronetage and read excerpts about her relations, as her brother is a baronet with four names hyphenated. Mr. B., the remittance man, came in, having "drink taken". Among other things, he said that anyone who wrote a diary every day must be a bloody fool. This startled me and for a moment I wondered whether he knew I did, but that of course is impossible. Mary was inspired by the du Plat Taylors' researches into the baronetage to talk about various titled people she knew, but Mrs. du Plat Taylor greeted this with a veiled smile.

Eric Smith had the nerve to say to Cynthia tonight that the canned beef we had for supper had gone off. She just looked absolutely wooden and said nothing.

August 13 (four days later)
I have not written this diary for several days as I have been so sleepy every night that I could not keep my eyes open. Mine is quite a routine now, singling turnips and transplanting cabbages in the morning, stumping trees in the afternoon, fishing in the evening. At last I am catching on to fishing and got two salmon yesterday, biggish but not as big as Eric's, who got one of thirty-five pounds.

I have been seeing a lot of Cynthia as we do stumping and go fishing together. I do like her. She would be a wonderful girl to have with you in an accident as she never loses her head. She doesn't say much but one feels how genuine she is. Of course, our tastes are different. She loves dogs and her ambition is to have kennels of her own.

Today, as a reward for my industry, or because the turnip singling is finished and they don't know what to do with me, I am to go off alone overnight with Eric on a camping trip.

It was adventurous of the du Plat Taylors to come so far from home and try to start a new life, and they don't care about discomfort, bad food, or flies and are willing to work all day or oversee others. They must be a bit like the early English settlers in Canada, but they are out of date. They should have lived at the time the Empire was being founded. Mrs. du Plat Taylor could run an Empire single-handed.

August 14

In the morning we set out, Eric and Mr. B. (Eric had not told me that he was to join us) and myself. We hopped on a freight train to Fishells. The train bumped and swayed along. We were joking and singing. At Fishells Eric saw a railway worker wearing the tie of his Guards regiment and went up and spoke to him, thinking he must have been in the regiment, but he said he had bought the tie at Stephenville.

We camped beside the swirling salmon river opposite some white cliffs. Then we set off through the woods blazing a trail and climbed a steep cliff covered with thick undergrowth and dead trees and ferns that clogged our path. Eventually we reached the top, and from a sort of lair among the ferns and undergrowth we saw below us a great valley of green forest waving in the breeze and pierced by the broad sweep of the river. I felt like an explorer I have seen in some movie lying there peering into the wide, endless horizon. Eric said this would be the ideal place for his house. He is now talking of settling in this country. When we got back to the tent we covered the floor with spruce and lit our stove to keep the flies away. It got terribly hot inside the tent and we sat talking. They were drinking whisky. I had one. They said why didn't I join them and buy some land in Newfoundland. It is going for thirty cents an acre in these parts, but you have to sign an agreement to clear a certain proportion every year. I think I will. I have five hundred dollars of my own and for that I could be a landed proprietor and come to survey my broad acres.

Eric and Mr. B. went on talking and drinking for hours. I tried to sleep but it was so bloody hot from the stove that I could not get to sleep. Then I woke up about four in the morning and it dawned on me that I was getting bored with Eric's talk and his changing schemes and I thought bitterly how quickly one loses one's illusions about people. I shall always go on liking Eric, but I thought him so exceptional, such a man of the world, but he is only like a grown-up schoolboy. It is not his fault. He is the same but my view of him has changed.

August 15
It seemed interminable taking down the tent and stowing our stuff in our bags. It was very hot and flyey and we were all quite silent, in contrast to our high spirits yesterday. Then we caught the train and got back to Black Duck. I am not really so keen on camping.

August 16
A letter from Mother today. Life goes on much the same at home. William drunk again. Also, Roley has fallen completely under Katherine's spell. I am sorry for him if he has. I have hardly thought of her since I have been here.

Singling turnips all morning and in the afternoon Cynthia and I started off to go blueberry-picking. We had hardly set out when Mary issued out of the house and said that she would join us. So we set off for the blueberry barrens, which are on top of a cliff. There were no blueberries, so we had tea there and Mary never stopped talking for an instant. She is a good sort but is certainly somewhat thick-skinned and optimistic about her company being always welcome. Eventually she went home and Cynthia and I went trout-fishing. My casting is slowly improving and each day there are fewer blackflies. I don't think I have made much, if any, impression on Cynthia, but it is hard to tell as she is so extremely reserved. Today she was, for her, really forthcoming. Although no beauty, she looks delightfully fresh and fair and young. She is just one year older than me almost to the day, but she despises so many things and people too. She has no use for laziness or showing-off or new-rich people, and today she said how cowardly it was for people to commit suicide. What she despises may be despicable but I am not much good at despising.

Captain G. came to dinner. He is an ADC at Government House in St. John's, a charming but very deaf young retired Guardsman with a monocle. He brought a friend called Captain N. who has a place near here. He had a mane of tawny hair and looked like a photograph of Rupert Brooke, but he is far from poetical as he is mainly interested in racing, at which he lost most of his money, so he decided to start afresh here. He says he can always pop over to his club in London if he gets too bored. There is quite a colony of retired army and navy officers scattered about here. They all come under the inspiration of Captain Campbell, the explorer, who is their idol, and I don't wonder. He is an exceptional man, the finest of a fine breed, so modest and yet with some quality about him so that you would follow him anywhere. He brought his wife here to join him but she could not stand the flies and went home. His son is here with him, a young man with a determined jaw.

August 17
Cynthia and I went stump-clearing in the morning but it was so hot that after a time we sat down in a clearing, made some cocoa, and discussed missionaries, and marriage, what we would do if we had four thousand pounds a year, and a few other things. Then we decided not to go back for lunch but to go fishing instead. There was a fresh breeze and we lay at anchor in the trout brook fishing from the boat. The breeze stirred the foliage on the banks and there were no flies (no fish either). It was delightful to have a hot sun on one's face and feel the even swing of the boat under one, and finally we both fell asleep.

August 18
A day of departures. Eric suddenly announced that he was leaving tomorrow. I have thought for some days that he was getting bored here. I was just reflecting while doing some land-clearing how much I would miss him when Mary came out and joined me and said would I go for a walk with her as she had something to tell me. So we started out down by Trout Brook. She seemed somewhat embarrassed and finally came out with it that the du Plat Taylors really only wanted me for this one month. They had originally said two. I must say I was quite upset but I tried to treat it casually. I don't know why they couldn't tell me themselves instead of sending Mary as their emissary. I know I have no knack for manual work but I have certainly tried hard. However, I see the du Plat Taylors' point of view. Why should they give me board and lodging if I am not worth it? They have been extremely kind, making me feel quite one of the family. I wonder if Cynthia has known these last few days that we have been together about my coming departure.

Mary then said that she was going back with me, so perhaps she has had a strong hint too that she has, as Jane Austen puts it, "delighted them long enough".

Eric left today. I walked with him along the track to the Black Duck station. We discussed when to wear dinner jackets and when white ties. He said when I came to England I must be sure to look him up and took my arm affectionately. I felt suddenly very sad to see him go and could hardly face him to say goodbye.

When I got back Mrs. du Plat Taylor announced that we were all going to take the afternoon off and go on a picnic to Fawsley Plain, which is a rocky point in the river. So we paddled upstream and then walked. Colonel du Plat Taylor walked ahead with me and was very nice, thanking me for all I had done. He said they would have been happy to keep me longer but had other visitors arriving from England and needed the tent.

We took a long time to decide where it was best to have the picnic and our choice was unfortunate, as no sooner had we sat down on our coats in the sun and Mrs. du Plat Taylor was making cocoa than we were surrounded by a swarm of wasps. They seemed to concentrate on the ladies of the party. Then Mary gave a scream and said, "There are wasps in my long boots." They had got into the rubber boots she was wearing to wade in and were biting her feet. So Cynthia and I hauled off her boots and she sat back on the rocks quite frustrated. Mrs. du Plat Taylor calmly said, "I think there are some in my long boots too," and when her boots were pulled off her feet and legs had been bitten worse than Mary's, but she had never said a word about it, much less screamed. What a woman! Then Mary said she had always been peculiarly sensitive to insect bites, at which Mrs. du Plat Taylor looked quite pitying.

At supper in the evening we had cider as a special treat and I wore a bow tie of Eric's which he had given me.

August 27

These last days at Black Duck have merged into each other, days of hard manual labour, singling and transplanting in the mornings, land-clearing in the afternoons, trout-fishing in the early evenings, three meals a day plus tea, such an appetite and thirst that I could eat hunks of bread and drink gallons of water, and would fall into bed in my tent at night and by the time I had read a page by the light of my gas lantern I was asleep.

In these last days I have seen a lot of Cynthia, but if there was a tremor of attraction between us it seems to have settled down into a kind of common-sensical friendship. Mrs. du Plat Taylor has become increasingly gracious as our departure draws near. In fact, she and I have had a number of tête-à-tête chats while I was hoeing and she stood beside me composedly in her sweeping serge skirts and in boots, with her hair in a bun. She is far from being a fool, but blinkered by prejudice. I realize now that her old-fashioned style of dress makes her look timeless, but she must be considerably younger than Colonel du Plat Taylor, who remains polite and unapproachable behind the barrier of out-of-date copies of *The Morning Post,* or measuring the land limits draped in his overhead mosquito net. The day Mary and I left, the whole family came to Black Duck to see us off.

Slowly the train jostled on to Port-aux-Basques and I saw the last of the countryside. The green forests and flashing rivers and prehistoric stretches of marsh and barren lands, and the blue mountains in the distance. I have developed a feeling for this country and the Newfoundlanders themselves. They live as they did in the eighteenth century and have not met with democracy, compulsory education, or the motor-car. This gives the people in the fishing villages a character of their own.

We embarked on the boat at Port-aux-Basques. The crossing was very rough and I was so sick that although I saw plenty of bedbugs and was stung by them too I didn't give a damn but finally got to sleep exhausted.

I was awakened by Mary's voice making loud and voluble enquiries after my welfare and the next thing I knew she had barged into the cabin, surprising my cabin mate, who was in the middle of dressing and just had time to pull on his pants. Mary, nothing daunted, began a long conversation with him and discovered that he was an ex-N.C.O. in the Black Watch. I can quite see how Mary has always been so popular with the Navy in Halifax all these years. They all know her, from admiral to midshipman, and the name Mary Binney is familiar in Malta and Mauritius. Last night she had slept in her clothes and her black matted hair looked, as Eric used to say, "as if it had been worried by a rabbit". She is a cheery old girl and I have got extremely fond of her. We have been through a lot together at Black Duck.

Altogether I would not have missed my time in Newfoundland for anything. I feel it has changed me and in spite of my failure as a farm worker it has given me new confidence and I am really grateful to the du Plat Taylors for putting up with me.

September 1

Geraldine has arrived from Boston to stay with us and Roley and I went down to the station to meet her. I haven't seen her since she was thirteen, and I certainly got a surprise when this glamorous apparition came mincing along the platform with quite the air of an actress condescending to arrive in a hick town. She had on a big black hat "framing", as they say in novels, "her aureole of red-gold hair". In the afternoon we all went to a tea-party at the Almons'. There was a thunderstorm and Colonel Almon was rather cross and slammed the windows to keep out the pouring rain so that it was as hot as hell in the drawing-room. Geraldine was making quite an impression, talking most entertainingly in a sophisticated way and smoking endless cigarettes from a long holder. Katherine, who was there, seemed quite like a child in comparison to her. In the evening Eileen, Roley,

95

Geraldine, and I went to the Mitchells' dance. It was in their house for a change instead of a club, and went swimmingly, especially as the Mitchell brothers are very kind and polite about looking after any of the girls who might feel left out from not having enough partners, especially Miss Ferguson. I braced myself to ask her for a dance. It was sheer hell. She hops about like a flea when she is dancing. Geraldine certainly did not have any problem for lack of partners. She was the sensation of the party in a clinging white dress covered with sequins. Katherine was there dancing with Tommy. She was swaying in and out of his arms as they danced as if she was drunk but I know she never drinks anything. Her face was flushed and she looked under an enchantment, as if the other people in the room were not there at all. When I spoke to her between one of the dances she clasped my hand in her hot hand and rubbed her face against my face, saying, "Hello, dear. I haven't seen you for ages." It was as if she was talking in her sleep. When we came home and the others had gone to bed Geraldine and I were standing about in the hall talking about the party and I, unexpectedly to myself, kissed her. I had had no intention of doing so an instant before and it was not what they call an uncontrollable impulse. It was more the way she moved restlessly about in the hall, picking up a gramophone record and putting it down again, lowering her lids and giving me a kind of indifferent glance and not replying to my chatter. It made me feel as though we were on stage and that I had a part to play and was missing my cue. The moment I kissed her I felt that I'd made a blunder. She went quite rigid, pushed past me, and ran upstairs.

September 7
I woke up this morning feeling that I had made a fool of myself last night and wondering how Geraldine would behave. When I came down to breakfast she was at the table talking to Mother and Roley. She did not answer

when I said good morning and while I was eating my eggs and bacon she went on talking to Mother. As we were going out of the dining-room into the hall I mumbled some incoherent excuse for my conduct but she didn't answer and only gave me a kind of insolent stare. I went up to my room and tried to settle to reading Bryce's *Holy Roman Empire* but I was too keyed up to care about the mediaeval kings and their remote trials and triumphs. I was asking myself what my strategy should be; after all Geraldine is staying here for a whole week and I cannot go on trying to pretend that nothing has happened and be natural if she continues to behave like this. Then I asked myself what my Uncle Charlie would have done and so when Mother had gone out and the coast was clear I went down to the library where Geraldine was sitting on the sofa turning over the pages of an old magazine. I sat down beside her and told her that the moment she had come into the house I had been carried away by her beauty and was now madly in love with her. Then she took the floor and, crying faintly into her handkerchief, told me that she forgave me and that she had always since she was a young girl been secretly fond of me but that pride had prevented her showing it. We then fell into each other's arms and remained thus until the others came back for lunch. How much either believes the other is a difficult point; even more difficult is how much what we said we are now beginning to believe.

In the evening a lot of people came out here: the Robertsons, the Almons, Tony, etc., etc. We played clock golf in the drawing-room.

In the morning my bedroom was housecleaned and I found that this diary had been moved from its usual place and that the pages were all mixed up, so I have a horrible suspicion that someone has been reading it, but who? Perhaps my mother, but would she be bothered? I could never face anyone who had read my diary. All afternoon Geraldine and I sat smoking and petting on the sofa. Certainly any experience of sex I ever had be-

97

fore was quite milk and water compared to this. She confided a complication in her life which perhaps explains a great deal, and that is that she is engaged to be married to a man in Boston named Ed and that the marriage is supposed to take place next year. She says that she only got engaged to him in a fit of pique though not in the least in love with him. She says that if she was free she would marry me. I remember that when we were both children we used to have a passion for acting charades and forced the other children to play bit parts in the performance while she and I were the hero and heroine. Are we acting a charade now with the library sofa as a prop?

This afternoon I felt I had to get away from Geraldine for a time and went for a walk by myself. As I was passing the Ritchies' house I saw Cousin Eliza sitting in the garden with her eyes closed, looking very calm like a corpse. I though I'd take a chance and ask her to explain Spinoza to me. I have been reading Spinoza for the last two weeks for my political science course. I am absolutely fascinated by him. He is such a relief after the horrors of Hegel and Kant and the Germans, with his limpid style and complicated reasoning. When Cousin Eliza was younger she wrote a book about Spinoza. I jumped over the stone wall into their garden and joined her and began very cautiously to mention the subject, not wanting to say anything silly, and she puckered up her eyes and stared in front of her and then said in a dry voice, "You are asking the right questions in the wrong way," and that was all. It was very discouraging.

September 11

I decided not to wear my glasses all day in the hope of changing my appearance and my personality. Mother asked me if I had lost them but I said airily, "No, only misplaced them." She just raised her eyebrows.

Geraldine is out for the day. I walked into town to buy a hat as I have lost my old one. Walking along Inglis Street I met Katherine, who had just got off the tram.

She looked so changed, her face pale and puffy. As I walked along she told me that Tommy had gone abroad for a year to stay in France. She looked miserable as she said this. I thought she was going to cry. I felt sorry for her. I did not think the day would ever come when I would feel sorry for Katherine. When I got home I went to my room and read *Saint-Simon's Memoirs*. It is just like having a courtier of the reign of Louis XIV in the room talking to you.

Then I began reflecting about Geraldine and myself. There have been moments when I thought I loved her but the feeling always fades. My real feeling about her is mainly vanity; I am proud of being seen with her because the other boys envy me and it puts up my stocks. When we are together I pretend to be a lover in a movie and imagine how he would behave, and by acting I become passionate and put on a performance. I think she is doing the same — acting a heroine. Sometimes we forget our lines or run out of them and as there is no prompter behind the scenes we just have nothing natural to say to each other, and there are awful pauses when I feel like saying, "Oh, do go away and let me read a book in peace," but of course I can't say that, so I burst into forced speech and end up telling her some long story about William and the stables or saying how much I love her, so then we begin making love again to fill in time. Sometimes I glance at my wrist watch, hoping she doesn't notice, and I am always surprised to find that we have been together such a short time when it seemed a century.

September 15
I got my exam reports today for all the subjects (except maths, in which I had to take supps.). They are: firsts in classics, firsts in political science, firsts in government, only seconds in English and French. This is very peculiar because I am much more interested in English than I am in classics or government, and expected to do better in it.

In the morning Roley and I went for a ride. We had a really good gallop, which you can hardly ever get out of these livery-stable horses. It was gloriously exhilarating but when I got home my bottom was sore from riding in flannel trousers.

Geraldine is leaving here today to stay with the Kennedys and I must say it is a relief to me. I am tired of talking about the kind of love I don't feel and making the kind of love I do feel.

Anan has arrived to stay. She used to be my father's secretary and before that Roley's governess and so she is like a member of the family. She has had her hair shingled, which is a great mistake. In the evening we played bridge. It was not very successful as Mother got into an argument with Mary Binney. I don't know how she managed it as Mary just keeps on agreeing and agreeing and agreeing. After that we abandoned bridge with some ill feelings all around. Then Anan told our fortunes. Tony says he distrusts Anan's fortunes, which always contain "the offer of a well-paid salary with family discussions connected with it". He says he cannot imagine why there would be any discussion about a well-paid salary.

September 17
Katherine telephoned me this evening and asked me to come and see her as she had something to tell me. When I got to the Almons' they were all out and the children in bed upstairs. Katherine met me in the hall. I noticed that she had on my signet ring, which she has not worn for a long time. We went into the big empty drawing-room and turned on the lights and sat down side by side on the stiff sofa. I had not seen her to talk to for weeks and I felt as though we were acquaintances who had met at a tea-party. Then she said, "This will be a surprise to you and I am telling no one but you because I am very fond of you and am afraid I have often been beastly to you. I am going to be married." I was thinking, "I suppose it's Tommy," but she went on, "To an older man." Before I

could stop myself I said, "Not David Martineau?" "Yes," she said, "How did you guess? He has written proposing to me. I sent him a letter today accepting. I am going out to British Columbia next month to join him on his farm." I thought, "She is not in love with him." I was completely certain of it. I know what she is like when she is in love and when she is not in love. All I could think of to say was, "I hope you will be very happy." "Now," she said, "you must take back your ring. Remember you said it was only a loan? Anyway we were never really engaged, were we?" She took off the ring and handed it to me. I put the ring in my pocket and went out into the hall. As she was opening the front door she turned and kissed me on the lips. I began trembling and felt a sob coming and said, "Don't do this. You know I love you," and she said, "Yes, I know you did but you are going to Oxford and that's what you always wanted. Don't worry about me. I'll be all right." As I walked down the drive I started crying and could not seem to stop. It is such a waste — a waste of her life to marry this old crackpot, a waste of my love for her, a waste of everything. I would far rather she had married Tommy, but I suppose he did not ask her. Of course, as she said, we were never really engaged, and she never loved me, and I did not love her enough to give up Oxford, but I did love her and no one else.

September 22
Tomorrow is my nineteenth birthday. My life is slipping away so fast. I shall be an old man before I have accomplished anything. This time next year I shall be at Oxford. One chapter finished . . . another begun. I can't help seeing my life as a book and myself as a character in it. Here everything is changing: Peter gone to Cambridge, Katherine soon away and married to Martineau. I hardly ever think of Katherine now. It would be like trying next morning to remember a dream you had the night before — you just cannot concentrate on the memory.

The biggest change and the saddest one is that The Bower is to be sold. Mother cannot cope with the expense of it any longer. I cannot believe that anywhere else will ever be home to me again.

PART 2

OXFORD
1926-1927

September 22, 1926

I have been re-reading my last year's diaries. How long ago all that seems. I think I have grown up in this last year. I have worked much harder at college, but have I changed? I can only hope so. It would be too awful to remain the way I was then. Anyway, everything else around here has changed: Peter at Cambridge, Tony back in England, Katherine away and married to Martineau. (I have had one note from her since she left, enclosing a snapshot of herself. She looks different, but it may be a bad snapshot.) The biggest change is that I leave for Oxford in two weeks' time. It is actually going to happen. Every time I think of it a kind of tingling of excitement goes through me and I cannot sit still in one place. I shall be a different person when I get there as there will be no one there who knows what I have been like till now. It will be a new page with nothing written on it, and the beauty of Oxford itself, the knowledge to be absorbed, the exchange of ideas and impressions with brilliant witty new friends — all this wonderful opportunity is thanks to my mother who is making so many sacrifices to find the money for my allowance and the college fees. I owe everything to her and I shall never forget it.

I find in my diaries how often I have written that I was restless and discontented here. How I have wanted to get away. Now that I am going I begin to think how much happier I have been than I have realized at the time, and how much I shall miss this beloved house, my home, The Bower.

October 2

On board ship. The first day up after four consecutive days and nights of seasickness. How this boat rolls and pitches. I don't know which is worse, the shuddering roll or the vicious pitch that half throws you out of your berth. It is a small boat, 9,000 tons, and the steward says the weather off the Grand Banks is the worst they have had for years. It is the season of equinoctial gales. I have spent my time being sick, recovering from being sick, and waiting to be sick again.

If I open my eyes I see my overcoat swaying as it hangs on the hook and that is enough to start me off again. I haven't even thought of Oxford. I have sincerely wanted to die. I have nothing to read but J. M. Barrie's *The Little Minister* and if I ever see it again it will make me seasick. A kind cross-eyed steward brings me brandy and tells me not to go near the dining-saloon, where he says the passengers are "stoofing themselves with dookling and vomiting all over the place".

October 4
Walked on deck. How this boat stinks! They have just been painting the old crock and even the funnels smell of fresh white paint. Then there is the smell of frying grease coming through the grills from the galley. I try to forget the smells walking around with Dr. Grenfell, the medical missionary in Labrador, a most magnetic and idealistic man. When I heard of the hardships of the people and snow blindness, etc., I felt ashamed of making a fuss about seasickness, but still I felt decidedly queasy.

October 5
Weak and empty as an old paper bag, but better. I got into conversation with a graduate student, also on his way to Oxford. He is a fine intelligent young man called Forsey. He has read all the serious articles in political science magazines and attended sessions of the House of Commons in Ottawa and taken notes of the proceedings. He will probably be a figure in Canadian public life. Why can't I be more like him?

October 9
There is a plump girl or young woman with black curly hair, cut short, who has the next chair to me on the promenade deck. We have been chatting together for the last day or two over the watery cups of bouillon the deck

stewards pass round in the morning. She is going to study at the London School of Economics and has written a thesis on Guild Socialism. She seems very earnest, but this morning she pressed my hand under the steamer rug. After dinner I asked her into the smoking-saloon and we had a couple of brandies each. I am getting quite addicted to brandy since I got aboard this boat.

Then we went up on deck. There was a rough sea and we slithered about the wet deck arm in arm and came to stop against one of the funnels. The boat was rolling so much that our embrace was almost impossible, but not quite. All she said afterwards was, "Oh, I have got white paint on my coat." Then we went in and had another brandy and she began talking about Guild Socialism again as though nothing had happened.

October 10
There was a heavy fog as the boat came up the Mersey and we hung about in the river for what seemed hours. When the fog lifted I missed the first glimpse of England as I was down in my cabin trying to calculate the amount of the tips I should give to the different stewards: the cabin steward, the deck steward, the dining steward, etc. I should like to give the whole lot to my cabin steward; he probably saved my life with the brandy when I was seasick.

In Liverpool it was raining. I took the cross-country train to Cheltenham to stay with great aunt Zaidée. It was a long trip. I had a carriage to myself and pressed my face to the window gazing at the flooded fields and trying to feel excitement at being here at last, but I was longing for a pee and it was not a corridor train. I thought I should burst but fortunately the train stopped long enough at some station en route for me to get out and back in again.

When I got to Aunt Zaidée's house it was past midnight and she had gone to bed, which was disappointing as I had looked forward to talking to her, but she is old

— eighty-seven — and has not been well. Her maid, Elizabeth, waited up for me. She has been with Aunt Zaidée since she was a girl forty years ago and is a wonderful woman, highly intelligent. Mother says that if she had had a chance she would have been capable of running a successful business of her own, but she seems completely devoted to Aunt Zaidée.

I was exhausted when I got to bed and half wished I was back at The Bower.

October 11
It is odd being back in this house where I have not been since I was a boy on my first visit to England ten years ago. Nothing has changed here: still the same three maids and the same cook whose husband, the coachman, taught me how to ride a bicycle circling round the flower beds on the gravel path in this garden. Aunt Zaidée came down to the drawing-room this morning after breakfast. She has hardly changed either. She has been a charmer and she still is with her soft voice, the sparkle of her blue eyes and her rose-leaf complexion, encouraged by touches of rose-leaf rouge worn in an old-fashioned way high up on her cheeks. She has little ringed hands. On one finger she wears a ring made of three bands of stones: each band is the engagement ring given her by each of the three husbands she has outlived — the first, from the days of her Nova Scotian girlhood, was a gambler and a bankrupt; the second, a bishop; the third, a general. When she came to England she changed her name from plain Sadie to exotic Zaidée. She has had no children and thinks of my mother as a loved daughter. I wish I felt more at my ease with her. I never have since I was a boy, when she could not conceal her distaste for my hay fever, my eyes oozing, a dripping nose, uncontrollable sneezing fits. She likes people to be seemly and decorative and makes me feel doubtful whether I am either.

When she had gone up to her room I paced about the drawing-room among the small tables and bric-a-brac, and when I was peering at some miniatures hanging on a velvet screen behind the sofa I managed to knock over the screen, and the miniatures came clattering down all over the floor. I pinned them up again, I hope in the right order, as I am sure Aunt Zaidée would notice if they were not. Then I went into the pantry and sat drinking tea and joking with the maids. One of them, Sarah, was always my favourite. She is so gentle, just the sort of woman I should like to be married to.

October 13
I left Cheltenham this morning to go to stay with the Lauries. When I said goodbye to Aunt Zaidée she gave me a cheque for £50, so I take back anything critical I thought about her. She is a Grand Old Girl. The Lauries are great friends of Mother's and are extremely kind to me. Colonel Laurie is full of life and enthusiasm, like a young man. He took me on a tremendous walk today across the Epsom Downs and walked so fast that I could hardly keep up with him. He is very religious and evangelical — a fine man. He does not approve of drinking or smoking, so I go and sit in the conservatory when I want to smoke. I have been talking quite a lot to Mrs. Laurie. She is so understanding — I feel I can say anything to her — a really Christian woman, but she never forces her faith on you. She is lovely to look at too: beautiful brow and eyes.

October 14
The Lauries motored me to Oxford today. I was really shivering with excitement and hardly knew what I was saying when we were talking in the car. It was raining and we took some time to find my digs, which are in the Abingdon Road. It was a wrench saying goodbye to the Lauries. They are the last link with home. My digs consist of a bedroom and half a sitting-room, the latter to be shared with an American Rhodes Scholar. The sitting-room looks out on now flooded playing-fields. There is an

aspidistra in the window and a small fireplace with one log smouldering in it. The landlady is very toothy and genteel. Her husband, who is a plumber, lurks in the back hall. When I was unpacked the Rhodes Scholar came in. His name is Post. He has a round, pink face and is quite old — a graduate student from the Western States. He looks good-natured but was very firm with the landlady about putting more coal on the fire.

I do not have to report in to college till tomorrow morning, so tonight I walked along the Abingdon Road and over the Folly Bridge into Oxford and turned left opposite Christ Church to where I had been told Pembroke College was — *my* college — and went into the porter's lodge. It was crowded with undergraduates talking and laughing together in groups and I felt very out of it not knowing anyone. I asked the porter where I could have dinner and he said Hall was not open till tomorrow "but some of the gentlemen go to the George Restaurant," so I followed his directions and came in to a little bar packed with undergraduates who seemed more smart and glossy than the ones at the porter's lodge at Pembroke. They were making a lot of noise chaffing each other and standing each other drinks and telling stories of what had happened to them in the vacation. I ordered a cocktail and sat down in a corner watching the animated scene. Then I had another cocktail and I thought, "Here I am, friendless in a city of friends," so I had a third cocktail and said to myself, "Some day I will come back to this bar surrounded by friends of my own," but I couldn't face going up to the restaurant and having dinner alone so I walked back to my digs and on the way looked through the porch of Christ Church at the noble, spacious quad, the lighted windows gleaming through the damp mist, and I felt a pang of pleasant excitement and anticipation heightened by the cocktails taken on an empty stomach. When I got to my digs Post was in the sitting-room drinking a glass of beer. He said, "You and I will have to come to an arrangement with these people about having sufficient coals and firewood. This place is cold enough to freeze your balls off." I must say he is right; it is damned cold.

October 15
This morning I reported to Drake, the senior tutor. I was ushered into a sort of sitting-room, where all the other freshmen were sitting about looking self-conscious and pretending to read magazines. Drake looks ageless as an icon and just about as welcoming. (I believe he is one of the last surviving dons who came in under the old rule that dons could not marry.) He was grimly polite to me but when he looked at my credentials he seemed very doubtful whether King's College, Halifax, Nova Scotia, existed at all. Then he told me that I was to take no History in my first year but to do Pass Mods instead. I was too awed at the moment to protest but I have every intention of doing History as I always planned. Our next interview was with the Dean. I had expected a potbellied, old grey-beard, but he can't be forty. He has an aureole of golden curls, a most seraphic smile, and a positively caressing manner. He had actually heard of Nova Scotia and thought he had a cousin there, either there or in British Columbia.

I dined in Hall and sat next to a red-haired man called Ducker with a prominent jaw. I made the mistake of remarking on the effect of the evening light coming through the coloured windows on the panelling and portraits. He lowered his head in a disapproving silence. After dinner when we were walking across the quad he told me that it was not good form to make such comments. The beauties of Oxford are supposed to be taken for granted. Still, he doesn't seem such a bad sort. We were joined by another freshman called Miles, a dark-eyed, untidy youth whose ambition is to become a Shakespearean actor. We three sauntered about the streets in the rain, trying to look as if we had been up at Oxford for at least two years.

October 16

I went to my first lecture today from the Dean on Voltaire as an historian. It was a most irritating performance. He pointed out the inaccuracies in Voltaire's historical writing and described it as "superficial", as if he was correcting an undergraduate's essay. I imagine that Voltaire could demolish the Dean with a flick of the wrist. In the evening Ducker and I adjourned after dinner to Miles' digs. He has photographs of actors stuck up everywhere. He knows all about Kean and Henry Irving and all the great Shakespearean actors, and he recited passages from Shakespeare with his dark eyes flashing. He has lent me *Hassan* by Flecker, a marvellous poem full of restless beauty. Later in the evening we went round to Hertford College to call on a friend of theirs called Johnson. He is a flaxen-haired, pipe-smoking man who has bought a lot of objects like bowls containing matches, etc., made of pebbly brown china with the Hertford arms emblazoned on them. The curtains were drawn and we sat round the fire drinking cocoa, at first talking seriously and then exchanging limericks. I walked home feeling that I had had a real Oxford evening.

October 20

I had tea with a group of Canadian undergraduates. It would be very easy to fall into the habit of going about with my fellow Canadians. There are quite a lot of them around and some very nice ones. Almost all are older than I am as they got degrees at colleges in Canada before coming here. Of course, it is nice to swap experiences of Oxford and to talk about things at home, but I did not come to Oxford for this.

Also, I have called on two or three boys who were at preparatory school with me in England, including John Martin, who was quite a friend of mine. He has become very conventional and seemed only moderately pleased to see me, saying that he expected that we might run into each other again sometime.

I am working hard on Stubbs and the *Gesta Francorum* and preparing for my first essay for my tutor McCallum at Pembroke, whom I like. He is a tall Scotsman with protuberant blue eyes, a great authority on Calvin. The truth is: at the end of a day's work I am lonely, if it wasn't such a humiliating thing to have to admit. The sitting-room in these digs is infested with American Rhodes Scholars, friends of Post's, who are very polite to me when I come in but then go on with their own conversation. I wish I could get rooms in college. The Dean says there is a chance I might.

October 22
This morning when I was sitting in my digs watching the rain come down on the wet playing fields opposite, the doorbell rang and a man named Morris came to call on me. He is the son of someone who knows the Lauries and so had heard of me. He seemed a modest little man with spectacles. He is a member of the Oxford Group, the Evangelical Religious group which is now so active. At first he talked uninterestingly enough of mundane things, but gradually he began to tell me of his struggles against temptation, against pride and impure thoughts, etc., and how the Oxford Group had changed his life. He had been on the verge of agnosticism but now he was happy as he had been brought to Christ. He said every morning he prayed for guidance for the day ahead, and more and more he received such guidance. In fact, he said he had been guided to come to see me, as he had been instructed that I was in need of help and might be struggling in the toils of sin and disbelief. He said that if I shared my burden with him it would become less hard to bear, and proposed that we might have what he called "a quiet time together". All this was said with such gentleness and good faith that I was quite moved and said what is true, that I had always had a great wish to believe but that it had quite dried up of late and that when I went to Communion I felt nothing. He asked me whether I would

come to an Oxford Group meeting, where I would find others like myself. I said that I would think it over but that I was not attracted to group meetings. He accepted this (apparently) and said that he would pray for me. I don't quite know what to make of this interview or of Morris or of myself. I don't, rationally speaking, believe in supernatural guidance, but then why should I trust my puny reason? It may be just a surface apparatus. Quite often when I am in trouble I call out "Oh, Christ". It may just be habit, or perhaps I do really believe in Christ, and the rest is what Morris calls spiritual pride. Also, I quite enjoy the opportunity to talk about myself and the state of my soul.

October 24
Tonight at dinner in Hall I sat next to an Egyptian called Matza. He has a profile like a film star, beautiful manners, and an eager smile. We took to each other at once and after dinner I went back to his rooms in the High Street. They are quite palatial, strewn with magnums of champagne, boxes of expensive French chocolates, and Egyptian cigarettes. A man-servant produced liqueurs for us. Later, some of Matza's friends dropped in: two Paris Americans, who from their talk live a kind of Ritz-bar existence, a lounging, pleasant fellow called Jeremy something, who somehow reminded me of Fabian Rockingham at home — the same careless charm — a man called Patterson who is at Pembroke and has just bought a racing car, and an Armenian called Sarkies with beautifully cut clothes and a black moustache, who has just come back from spending a weekend at Cookham with an actress. We had quantities of champagne and afterwards the man-servant set up a roulette table and we played. I lost fifteen shillings. I came home thinking, "This is the life for me, very different from the Johnson-Ducker set with their cocoa and limericks."

I was somewhat dampened to find a letter from Elizabeth, Aunt Zaidée's maid, saying that she hopes I don't mind her telling me that Aunt Zaidée had said, "Why does the dear boy address his letter to me as Mrs. Z. B. Prevost?" It was my letter to thank her for her cheque and I stupidly addressed it the way she signs her cheque instead of to Mrs. Prevost. She will think me a complete social ignoramus.

October 27

I dropped in to see Patterson, whom I met the other evening at Matza's. Although he is only a freshman, he has succeeded by sheer gall and persistence in getting some of the best rooms in this college: a noble panelled sitting-room next the porter's lodge in which he has installed a turkey-red carpet and hung up pictures of the lives of the cardinals in ye goode olde tyme in their scarlet robes, cracking nuts and drinking wine. He seems to want to match their style of living. On his sideboard were three outsize pineapples and a box of outsize Havana cigars.

He began by saying to me, "I am sure I can trust you to be completely frank. I have ordered three suits from Shepherds, and jolly expensive they were, and now Jeremy says that the coats don't fit, that the wind will whistle down the back of my neck where the coat collar stands off. Do you mind waiting while I put one on, and tell me what you think?" When he returned he was squeezed into a too-tight double-breasted suit of a colour I think called "electric blue". What Jeremy had said was perfectly true — the collar stood out a mile at the back. I had to say so. Patterson said, "What I don't understand is that Sarkies gets his suits from the same man and his clothes are always immaculate." Sarkies, that Armenian whom I met at Matza's, is Patterson's idol. He longs to be like him but I don't think he will ever succeed. In the first place he hasn't enough money. He says he is living already at double the rate of his allowance. (His family are not rich.) In the second place, no one could be less like an Armenian than Jim Patterson, but he wants to be the glamorous, high-living hero of a novel about Oxford, and an old-fashioned novel at that. He talked a lot about Jeremy, who he says is the younger son of the late Lord B. Patterson says that Lord B. died of shame when Jeremy was expelled from Harrow. He must have been a bloody old fool. Later on an old school-friend of Patterson's came in. He is at Trinity and I walked back there with him. He said that Patterson was a very good fellow but "afflicted with a glitter complex", and that he was quite well read but did not show it.

October 28

A Major Wilson came to call on me today. He had heard of me through Lewis, the Oxford Grouper. He is in the Intelligence Branch of the War Office and is at Oxford on a visit from London. He is a tall, thin, sallow-complexioned man of about forty with a military moustache. He was very interesting about the Balkans, where he spent some time as military attaché. He thinks there will be a communist revolution there one of these days and says the people at the top are hopelessly corrupt. He asked me what I intended to do when I came down from Oxford, and I mentioned that I might want to go in for diplomacy or to be a journalist if I could be a foreign correspondent. Major Wilson believes that the only answer to communism and materialism is the Christian faith, and that just as *they* have a faith we must have one too, and that the Oxford Group has the vitality that the church is losing. He asked me whether I was interested in the Oxford Group. I rather hedged and he looked at me very keenly and said, "I quite understand your doubts; for many years I shared them. In fact I was an atheist, but there is a spiritual power to be drawn on like any other kind of power if you know the way and the way is to put pretensions behind you and get back to the straight path of faith in Jesus." Then to my amazement he asked, "Would you pray with me?" and there and then went down on his knees. Of course I couldn't refuse, so there we were at 11 a.m. on an ordinary day: a distin-

116

guished military attaché and I, on our knees in my sitting-room in silent prayer. When he got up he returned to talking about the international situation without any self-consciousness. Then he said he must be off to catch the train.

I was impressed by Major Wilson and I liked him. He didn't talk a lot of stuff about purity and evil thoughts like Morris did. He seemed to combine simple faith with a clear mind. He did not make me feel awkward or embarrassed, and of course I am flattered that a man of his age and position should show so much interest in my spiritual welfare.

October 29

I read my first essay today to my tutor McCallum. It was on *The Origins of the French Revolution*. I had worked on it till I hated it. McCallum said, "It has promise; you can write English." Then he showed me his early editions of Calvin's writings and I pretended to be interested. He said, "A delightful young undergraduette will be arriving as you leave. You should meet her. I am tutoring her in economic history," and she did appear — a long, bony, pasty face with black wiry hair. I shuddered inwardly.

I am lucky to have McCallum as my tutor. He is stern but human. He admires P. G. Wodehouse almost as much as he does Calvin.

October 30

Patterson had a roulette party last night in his rooms. I lost nearly £20 which I cannot afford. Jeremy was there. He is a charming creature, loose-limbed, casual, and funny. Matza was there. I noticed that though he was the richest man in the room he made the smallest bets. Patterson and Sarkies were both wearing co-respondent shoes. I talked to a man called Anstruther-Gray who asked me to lunch next week. He is very noisy and talks a lot, tall with a small head and pretty, ineffectual features. I walked home with the Armenian Sarkies. He is a third-year man and he said, "They are nothing but a lot of schoolboys."

It is quite true that these English undergraduates do seem incredibly young. It's the way they have been brought up. For one thing, they have never had anything to do with girls except sisters and the odd girl they have met at a tennis party or a dance. They have never talked to a girl about anything. They are mostly virgins, though they would rather die than admit it, and they don't know anything about petting as we practise it at home. They talk about sex a lot but it is mainly smut and endless limericks. There don't seem to be any available girls at Oxford, only undergraduettes and whores. The only exceptions I have seen are a few stunning Scandinavian blondes who seem to be the preserve of a fortunate few. The undergraduettes are hardly regarded as girls. They are to be seen bicycling to lectures with unpowdered noses, wearing hideous regulation Tudor-style black velvet caps. At lectures they take down every word that falls from the lecturer's lips as though their lives depended on it. No one I know has ever penetrated to a women's college, although it is said that there are a few female wits and beauties there.

October 31
Morris called for me today to go with him to the Oxford Group house party which is taking place at Wycliffe College, the low-church establishment. These so-called house parties are really Oxford Group meetings to which people come from all over the world. When we got to Wycliffe there were about forty men gathered in the big panelled sitting-room. They were of mixed ages, some quite middle-aged and others about our age, mostly undergraduates. We were greeted by a giant with a blond beard called Loudon-Hamilton. He is apparently a well-known athlete who came down from Oxford a few years ago. He seemed very breezy and friendly. None of the people there looked like religious fanatics. Several of

them were naval officers. Some were foreigners: one or two Dutch and some Americans. The whole group looked well dressed, well washed, quiet, and gentlemanly. We sat about on chintz-covered chairs and sofas having tea. More and more people kept arriving until the room was quite full and there wasn't enough space for everyone to sit down. I found myself perched on the arm of a sofa. After a time of ordinary talk Loudon-Hamilton, who seemed to be the organizer, said "as usual" we would start the meeting by silent prayer for guidance, so we all crowded down on our knees and stayed there for some time during which my own mind was a complete blank. When we came to, Loudon-Hamilton gave a practical account of how the Group was doing, the new members, finances, plans for the future, the date and place of the next house-party. It was all very business-like and at the same time informal, like friends discussing a project in common. When that was all over Loudon-Hamilton said that it had always been found helpful for members of the Group to share with each other their struggles and temptations in coming to Jesus; that we could all learn understanding and compassion in this way, that some of us had already done this but other newer members or those who had just begun to hear the Call were now urged to tell of their own personal experience. I thought, "Suppose I am asked to share, what on earth shall I say?" First of all, an elderly man with a strong Scottish accent rose to his feet and gave a very long-winded account of his doctrinal difficulties in accepting a personal God. I thought he would never sit down. He went bleating on and on and I could see the others were as bored as I was. I began to long for a cigarette, but of course that was unthinkable. Then one after another stood up and told of their experiences. Some were moving and interesting, but there was one man who told of his struggle against fornication and how he had to fight off temptation and temptresses. He was quite fat with a pasty face and black hairs all over his hands and I couldn't help wondering what woman would be bothered tempting him. After that we had several men who told of their fight to attain Perfect Purity. I must say the audience quite woke up at this point, and I noticed Morris listening with a most peculiar expression on his face as if he was getting quite a kick out of this part of the proceedings. I began to think that there was a lot of showing off and boasting going on and that each one was trying to out-do the last one in describing the depths of his depravity and the torment of his remorse. I was simply amazed and really shocked to hear these nice quiet men, many much older than myself, standing up in their neat double-breasted suits and reciting these intimate things. But what finally put me off was that a young sublieutenant in the Navy got to his feet, quite red in the face, and said very awkwardly that his sin might not appear as great as some others but that he felt guilty not to confess it when so many had shared. It was that when he was at sea walking the deck on night-watch he was sometimes overcome with the desire to masturbate, that he looked up to the stars in heaven and prayed for strength to resist, but that to his shame he had sometimes given in. As he said this his voice broke and he began to sob. I was overcome with the most acute embarrassment and wanted to rush right out of the room. It was because he had not been showing off and he looked so wretchedly embarrassed himself. I closed my eyes so as not to look at him. However, someone patted him on the back and told him he had been very plucky to speak out and then to my horror Loudon-Hamilton turned to me and said in a quiet voice, "Would you like to share your burden?" I had suspected that this was coming but had been too much paralysed at the idea to have prepared any answer so I was tongue-tied. Although Loudon-Hamilton had spoken in a low voice, I could see the others were looking in my direction. At last I muttered that my sins had already been mentioned by other people and I had nothing to add at the moment. It was a most incoherent reply. Loudon-Hamilton said, "Come and make a clean breast of it; you'll feel much better afterward," but seeing the state of desperate self-consciousness and the kind of obstinacy that I had got into he put his hand gently on my shoulder and said, "No one is forced to share. Wait until you are guided." Then people looked away and someone else took the floor. I daresay that by the looks of me they felt they had not missed much in the way of a spectacular confession.

When I got back to my digs to-night I tried to think the whole meeting over. I do admire the sincerity of these people. I do believe that they are trying and perhaps succeeding in breaking away from the conventional Christianity, which is emptying the churches. I have been drawn towards their faith, perhaps more than I admit to myself, but I cannot and must not go on with it. It would be a fraud for me to continue. In fact, I have been a fraud, and the sin that I should have "shared", but which I can only share with this diary, is that I have encouraged Morris and the others by putting on an interested, believing look when I was listening to them, and all the time I have had no real intention of joining the Oxford Group and I never have believed in Guidance, although I may have wished for it.

November 1

I find Post, the Rhodes Scholar with whom I am sharing these digs, easy to get on with. He takes no interest in me nor I in him, and we do not get in each other's way. He is very easy-going except on one subject: the fire. The fire in the grate in the sitting-room is a very small fire in a very small grate. Each lump of coal that is added to it is brought in on a shovel by the plumber-landlord, who drops the lump with a heavy-laden sigh. This annoys Post. Yesterday he went into the hall where the coal scuttle is kept, picked it up, and emptied the whole contents on the fire. The landlady made a terrible fuss and said he had used up a whole week's coal supply and we would have to pay for it, but Post, shaking his head, said, "Not one cent." He said it so finally yet in such an affable tone that the landlady retired nonplussed.

In the afternoon I went to have tea with some Canadians, a mother and two daughters who have taken a house near here. The girls are not bad-looking, the sort I am used to meeting at dances at home, but they're Upper Canadians and think Toronto is the centre of the universe and that Nova Scotia is inhabited by fishermen and peasants. They brightened up when they heard that I had been at Trinity College School and their mother said that it was "the Eton of Canada". What damned nonsense!

November 2

That man Ducker has been telling me that I must take exercise, so today I turned out for soccer, having bought a soccer kit which was quite expensive. I cannot say I enjoyed the game. The ground was squelchy wet and there was an icy wind blowing. I haven't played since school and didn't want to make a fool of myself, so I rather hung around on the edges of the action, trying to imitate an eager player who longs to get the ball at his feet. However, when I got back to my digs and had a hot bath I felt very hearty and drowsy, quite the tired athlete.

November 3

This afternoon Morris called for me to take me to a tea party given by a Mr. Mercer of Wimbledon, who is staying here on a visit with his sisters in North Oxford. Mr. Mercer is a genial and earnest gentleman who held my hand for at least two minutes when I came in and looked benevolently into my face, which embarrassed me considerably. All the people there were, I think, members of the Oxford Group. They did not talk of religion but I could smell it in the air. Mr. Mercer handed round the teacups with an air of condescending humility, as if he were St. Louis washing the feet of the poor.

As I was walking home with Morris he produced out of

his pocket a piece of paper on which was a drawing of a key. The different parts of the key were labelled in his writing "Perfect Purity", "Perfect Faith", "Perfect Humility". He said he had a similar drawing of a key which he always carried with him and would like to give this one to me. He said he looked at his when assailed by temptation. I thought this puerile but somehow touching. He suggested that we should have a "quiet time" together once a week, but I draw the line at that.

November 4
As I was leaving the Oxford Union today, where I had been writing a letter to Mother on their free writing-paper, a small creature like a moth came fluttering down the steps beside me and burst into breathless conversation: "Oh, the sepulchral gloom of Oxford on Sunday afternoon. How does one survive it? One feels like going into the garden to eat worms. Don't you agree? I see you do. Come and have a cup of tea with me if you can bear my utterly squalid digs. The hideousness of them has to be seen to be believed." His name is Leslie Mahon. He lives in Wellington Square and his sitting-room is full of his landlady's antimacassars and Landseer steel engravings, to which he has incongruously added a large purple velvet pouf and some orange cushions and has pasted up reproductions of Bakst ballet costumes. When we got in he produced not tea but crème de menthe in tiny green glasses and curled himself up on the pouf. "To think you come from Canada," he said. "I have a grandmother there in Montreal. I stayed with her last winter. It is not a seat of culture and it is too penetratingly cold but she is so generous to one, such a dear understanding old person." Mahon wants to be a playwright and read me one of his plays. It was not very good and reminds me very much of Noel Coward's *Hay Fever*. Then he put Ravel's *Bolero* on the gramophone and we had some more crème de menthe and went on talking and the afternoon slid by quite entertainingly. It was dark when I emerged into Wellington Square.

November 6

In the afternoon I went to Jeremy's to play rouge-et-noir. His rooms are a glorious mess — mysterious bits of car engines, cigarette boxes, scattered playing cards, gramophone records, even packages of French safes are all left lying about in total confusion. It was a black rainy afternoon outside, so we drew the curtains, turned on the electric lights, and settled down to playing for five hours. Patterson and Anstruther-Gray and Matza were there. I lost again, this time £11 10s.

Afterwards we adjourned to the George Restaurant and Jeremy stood us to a sumptuous meal with unlimited burgundy. The restaurant was packed with undergraduates calling out to each other and wandering from table to table. It was a splendid scene of revelry, with the burgundy swimming about in one's brain and the George's punka swaying to and fro overhead wafting clouds of cigarette smoke. Mahon appeared, making quite an entrance as he was carrying a large Japanese painted fan and accompanied to my surprise by Roger Barclay, who is not at all the aesthete type but a sort of typical public-school boy, very handsome, which must explain it. Leslie Mahon kept waving to me with his fan in a coquettish way, which rather embarrassed me and led to a lot of jokes at my expense at our table. Towards the end of dinner Patterson suddenly began reciting the death-scene speech of Marlowe's *Dr. Faustus*, which he seems to know by heart, and flushed with burgundy he got to his feet and in a loud voice called out, "Christ's blood streams in the firmament." Jeremy said, "Go easy, old man," but Patterson just repeated it louder still until all the people round us stopped talking to listen. Finally we got him to sit down. He is an unexpected man, as a moment before he had seemed quite sober and had been talking about carburettors for his new car. When we got into the street we were all rather drunk. We saw a moving bus on its way to Headington and all jumped on and sat in the open seats at the top singing till the bus conductor asked us to stop as he said it annoyed the other passengers. That bloody fool Anstruther-Gray got into an argument with him, saying, "My good man, why don't you piss off." The bus conductor said, "How would you like a punch on the nose?" At that Anstruther-Gray yanked one of the wooden placards marked "To Headington" off and threw it into the street. Jeremy said, "Let's get off this bus pronto," so we clambered down and jumped off as it was going at a fast pace up Headington Hill. We had a long, cold walk back and Anstruther-Gray again distinguished himself, this time by being sick in the street. As we walked along together I said to Jeremy that I was fed up with Anstruther-Gray, but all he said was, "Poor bugger, he can't hold his drink." Jeremy is very good-natured, or nothing seems to matter to him.

November 7
A cold, blustery day. I woke up feeling unusually aggressive, so much so that I plucked up enough courage to go to see the Dean about getting rooms in college, and I was glad afterwards that I had done so as he said there was an unoccupied set of rooms over the porter's lodge that I might have on a temporary basis for a few months, but that after that he himself was going to move in there and use them for an office, and it was uncertain whether any other rooms could be found for me in college, so I might have to go back into digs. I jumped at this proposition, anything to get away for the time being from the aspidistra plants and the landlady with her genteel chat. Besides, these rooms used to belong to Dr. Johnson and still house his teapot.

In the evening to a roulette party at Matza's. Once again I lost. My bad luck is something phenomenal. I tried to imitate an Austrian gambler I have read about who remained impassive as the luck went against him by digging his nails into the palms of his hands until they bled. Jeremy said that my luck was bound to change and then he said he would stake me from now on and that when I won he would take fifty per cent of the winnings. This was very generous of him and I ought not to have accepted it, but I want to go on playing and I have no more ready cash at all until the next instalment of my allowance comes in. I am not a natural gambler and I started playing here because my friends do and I didn't want to be left out, but now it is beginning to take hold on me harder than on any of the others.

Later in the evening two prostitutes came in to join the party, just standing around and drinking gin. It was risky of Matza to have them in his rooms as of course no girls are allowed in digs at night, much less prostitutes, and one of them, Betty, is well known to the proctors. She is quite attractive in a coarse way. Somebody mentioned the name of Margot Poltimer, who is a kind of legend around Oxford for glamour, and Betty said, "The airs she gives herself, my lady Poltimer. She is nothing but a bloody tart and she spoils the market for the rest of us."

After the rest had gone home I stayed on with Matza for a final drink. He seems older in sophistication than the other undergraduates but he is rather lost at Oxford. People take advantage of his lavish hospitality and he is beginning to notice. I think he would be happier with others as rich as himself. He told me tonight that he had one ambition and that was to marry a beautiful, well-educated English girl — a blonde who understood the art of conversation. He says the nice girls he knows in Cairo are so strictly brought up that they know nothing, but he says that because he is an Egyptian no nice English girl will have anything to do with him; that they are polite enough at first meeting but that if he tries to go any further they freeze up. For example, he said he had a theatre party the other night in London and asked two English girls. They went on afterwards to a supper dance but both the girls made excuses and would not dance with him. He said that they don't want to be seen dancing with someone they consider coloured, so he said there is nothing left but prostitutes — "They don't care about colour except for the colour of my money." It is a rotten situation and I feel very sorry for him. Besides, he is so handsome and has such an air of distinction that I should think any girl would prefer him to most of the hobbledehoy youths around this place.

November 8
I have not seen anything of Morris for several days but he appeared at my digs today when I was out and Post was in. I think he must have made some kind of religious pass at Post because afterwards Post said to me, "Is that funny little guy all right in the head?" Morris had left a note for me saying that he'd made an appointment for me this afternoon to meet Bishop Taylor Smith, who he was sure could be of help to me. What nerve! Without consulting me beforehand, but I felt I had to go. The Bishop is a monstrously massive old man with a huge, somnolent head, and, surprisingly enough, quite a sense of humour, but when he weighed into religious subjects he talked to me as if I was a child or a private soldier. (He used to be Chaplain-General to the Forces.) He said he was first turned to Christ by the thought of the "riffraff" he would meet in hell, and then he wheezed out, "I am sure it would make you as a gentleman shudder to think of mixing with them." When I got out in the street I began laughing aloud to myself. I thought, "That has done it. I am through with the whole shebang — Morris and his key to Perfect Purity, and quiet times, and house parties, and sharing the burden of my sins."

November 18
I have not written this diary for ten days. During those ten days I have done no work. Each afternoon and every evening we have been playing rouge-et-noir and roulette and I have lost almost steadily. We usually gather in Jeremy's rooms, sometimes at Matza's. The curtains are drawn, the lights turned on, the air is thick with cigarette

smoke, half-finished glasses of whisky on the tables, a lot of loud talk. We always seem to play to music; someone puts on the gramophone, all those tunes, "Bye-bye Blackbird" with its melancholy note, "Blackbird . . . bye-bye", or a very old-fashioned tune, left over in Jeremy's rooms by a previous occupant, called "Roses of Picardy" or "Tea for Two, Two for Tea" jingling away. The needle gets stuck in the groove and grinds to a halt and someone gets up to wind the gramophone. The roulette wheel spins or the dice take a rattling fall on the bare boards of the table. The cards are dealt . . . vingt-et-un is my passion. . . ."I'll take a flip" . . . "I'll buy a card" . . . and another, and one more . . . that's buggered it . . . one over twenty-one. Roulette is a silly game — poker is not for me — but vingt-et-un is my passion.

This gambling is a real torment to me. It is such a waste of time and of my opportunities here at Oxford. It is the opposite of all I looked forward to. I used to think of the endless stimulus of Oxford and the interesting friends and the beauty of the place. Now I don't notice my surroundings at all, make no new friends, read nothing. My whole time is spent in this idiotic pursuit, and worst of all I have lost and continue to lose so much money — that is, much for me. To a rich man it would not seem much, but when I think of the sacrifices Mother has made to give me my allowance and the way I am wasting it, I am truly ashamed of myself. I should never have accepted the arrangement with Jeremy that he stake me for my losses. The result is that he has lost a great deal of money. He is so good-natured and generous that he never makes me feel uncomfortable about it, but it is a humiliating situation. What surprises me about myself is that I don't give a damn so long as I can keep on playing.

I had another letter from Mother today about the state of our finances. She says again that she will have to put The Bower on the market. She cannot afford to keep it up. Sell The Bower! It is such an awful prospect.

I went to McCallum today for my tutorial. After I had finished reading my essay he said, "You are a Scottish-Canadian, aren't you? Not a race, I think, to waste time and throw away opportunites in the way you are doing at present." I was somewhat taken aback but said that I intended to work much harder in the future. He said, "See to it," in rather a grim voice. In fact I intend to start afresh. Heaven knows how many "new lives" I have started in my day but this one is positively going to be different. To start with, I am not going to touch a card for the rest of this term, not even bridge at small stakes. Secondly, I am going to resume going to lectures, although I must say I do not get much out of them. Most of them are delivered by dons who have written books on the subject they are lecturing on so that the lectures are just regurgitated books, delivered usually in a very bored manner to a very bored audience. It is just as simple to read the book and skip the lecture. Thirdly, I have decided to read the *Gesta Francorum* twice a week with Ducker. In fact I can see him at this moment leaning his bicycle up in the porch and soon his elephantine step will be on the stairs. He is as heavy in mind as he is in body and terribly slow to work with. I have got fond of the *Gesta* and the school-boy Latin of the Crusaders' times and the figures in the history like kings and knaves in a pack of cards. Miles, the other man whom I met when I first came up here, seems to be offended with me. He has very nearly cut me several times in the quad. I don't think he approves of the company I keep.

From now on my days are going to be ordered on a system: so many hours' work, moderation in drinking, economy in spending, making friends who can stimulate my mind or help my career and discarding those who do not, watching my tongue, and not showing off.

I had a letter today from Elizabeth, Aunt Zaidée's maid, saying that Aunt Zaidée is seriously ill.

November 17

I have taken up boxing at the suggestion of Paton of Hertford, a very nice man I was at preparatory school with. I think it will keep me healthy and out of trouble, although it is a very unlikely pursuit for me. I went to his rooms today for the first lesson. I was pretty feeble, but I intend to stick to it and box three times a week, regularly. Paton thought I should see some real boxing, so we went this evening to the Oxford-versus-Navy match at the town hall instead of my going to Somerville to hear Harold Munro discuss poetry, which I had intended. I was quite amused at first but got bored after two or three bouts.

November 18

I saw in the newspaper today that my old school (or one of them) in Ontario has been burned down. I have no tender memories of that red-brick prison where I lost my faith "in God and Man". All the same I dropped in to see Mockridge, who is up here, and to bring him the news (which of course he had heard already). He is a very nice fellow, but I was surprised and annoyed to hear that he has invented a new reverse gear for motor-boats which he expects to bring him in £400 a year. What annoys me is that he is so well off already and doesn't need the money.

November 19

Patterson had a breakfast party in his room today — Sarkies, Jeremy, one or two others, and myself — we drank port with scrambled eggs and bacon. In the afternoon, feeling as sodden as the weather, I went for a walk to the Three Hinkseys with King, a New College man whom I am cultivating as I think it is time that I had a few scholarly friends and he is said to have "a first-class mind". He certainly has a lofty brow with receding chestnut hair, but he is damned dull company, and wore woollen half-mittens on his hands. He said he regarded sensuality and introspection as both being a waste of time. In the evening Mockridge took me to supper with Lady Osler, who is his aunt or cousin or something. She is the widow of the great Canadian doctor and lives in a huge Victorian Gothic house. She seems very kind but quick-tempered. I liked her. Her brother, Mr. Revere from Boston, was staying with her. He is a jolly old sod. Went home and read some of Squires' poems — very fine — and also Henry James' *The Awkward Age*.

November 20

I have at last met the famous Margot Poltimer, about whom there has been so much talk. Some people say that she is a gold-digger, others that she is "an enthusiastic amateur", and anyone who has slept with her feels that it is a great cause for boasting. Jeremy has known her since he was here at a crammer's, being tutored to come up to Oxford. Nobody seems to know exactly what has become of her husband, Brian Poltimer. One story is that when he was at Christ Church he married her for a bet after a Bullingdon Club dinner and when he woke up and found what he had done he vanished into thin air. According to another story he is lurking about somewhere, suffering from DT's. As for Margot herself, Jeremy says that she is the daughter of an Oxford landlady, convent-educated.

I was sitting in the George bar having a cocktail today when I saw this tall, leggy girl or young woman with a bleached Scandinavian look (the fashionable look of this year) coming in, pulling a miniature poodle after her on a lead. In about two minutes three or four men in the bar had gathered around her and I could hear her chattering away in rather an affected, actressy voice. Then that girl Vi came in to join her. She is Anstruther-Gray's girl, rather a dreary creature I think, but after a few minutes she came up to me where I was sitting and said, "You must be Cedric's friend. He has spoken of you so often that I feel I know you." I had never thought of Anstruther-Gray as Cedric. "Wouldn't you like to meet Margot? She is so attractive, isn't she?" So she took me up and introduced me and Margot said, "I crave a cock-tail, my sweet, a pink lady," so I ordered her one. The minute I heard her artificial way of talking I realized that she reminded me of someone. It is Geraldine, whom I knew at home; the same touch of the amateur actress, and I feel completely at my ease with her and strongly attracted. By now the bar was beginning to fill up and we were quite surrounded by a boisterous crew: some under-graduates and a man in a black and white checked suit with a carnation in his buttonhole who looked like a bookie, but Margot just went on talking to me as if we had known each other all our lives. She talks in a most affected way, moaning, "Vi and I had such a divine walk in the country today," and "I must have just one more teechy-weechy little cocktail." But underneath all this I feel that we understood each other, and asked her to lunch with me next week, which she immediately accept-ed, and then teetered out of the bar on her high-heeled shoes, dragging the poodle after her. Afterwards I dropped in to see Jeremy to ask him about her and he said, "Oh, she is a grand girl, Margot, but a bit careless about who she sleeps with." I asked about her husband and whether it was true he was dying of DT's and he said, "Old Brian Poltimer, not a bit of it. I was at school with him. Not a bad chap but infernally dull. He couldn't keep up with Margot at all, so he has buggered off to London and got some kind of a job. I believe he makes her some kind of allowance, not a very big one I should say."

November 21
When I opened *The Times* today I saw the notice of Aunt Zaidée's death, so I telephoned the house and talked to Elizabeth and am to go down to Cheltenham for the fu-neral tomorrow.

Today I moved into my new rooms in college. They are splendid, with a view up St. Aldates to Tom Tower. I am absolutely delighted with them, so much so that I could not sleep tonight but woke up, looking out of the window at the view of the church and the tower bathed in moonlight.

November 22

I went up to London today en route to Cheltenham and bought a black tie and an armband to wear at Aunt Zaidée's funeral. Then I dropped round to see Matza at a flat he has taken off Bond Street for his visits to London and found him and his cousin with two girls: one, a girl called Brima, is a Charleston dancer from a night-club. They were all in bed drinking champagne at ten in the morning. Matza began congratulating me on "my inheritance" from Aunt Zaidée and said to Brima, "You know he has just come into £15,000 a year." (Actually, of course, I haven't come in for a single cent so far as I know.) Brima said, "Well, I liked him before you said that. I like people for their own sake and not what I can get out of them." The other girl laughed and said, "You *are* a scream, Brima," and Brima said, "Oh, do shut up." The train to Cheltenham took hours.

I am staying at Pyatts Hotel where I stayed once before. It is a real survival of Dickens' days. After a solitary dinner I went over to Aunt Zaidée's house. Aunt Zaidée's maid, Elizabeth, took me into the drawing-room. She had her hair in a net and was wheezing with asthma. It seemed so odd and almost scandalous for us to be sitting there in Aunt Zaidée's absence. Elizabeth told me that in Aunt Zaidée's dying delirium she thought she was in a ward filled with smallpox patients and lying on a bed of broken glass. She also said that Aunt Zaidée had sewed up all her good jewellery in a pincushion to avoid tax collectors, and that this was to be told to mother as a secret, as the jewellery is left to her. Elizabeth has the pincushion in her bedroom.

November 23

Today the other relations gathered, not very many of them: two stepdaughters, each the wife of a son of Aunt Zaidée's two last husbands, one a very vague lady, the other somewhat beady-eyed. The vague lady never stopped talking, mostly about the evils of the younger generation, saying how much she disapproved of girls having their hair bobbed or Eton-cropped. She said a woman's greatest beauty is her hair: "When I was a girl, mine was so long that I could sit on it. Now you can hardly tell a girl from a man." She certainly has plenty of hair, hers done up with tortoise-shell combs, but it always looks on the verge of falling down. Mr. Collins was there. He is a sort of cousin of ours, exceedingly rich. Mother once sold him some family silver when she was particularly hard up. He is a soft-spoken, nervous little man of about fifty with small, useless-looking hands. He seems obsessed with the danger of communism and says that he expects any day now to see the communist mob at the gates of Dunloran, which is the name of his house in Kent. He was very friendly tonight and talked a bit about Oxford and the wild times he had had there when he was a member of the Bullingdon Club. It is hard to imagine him as a wild undergraduate. He asked me to go and stay with him but I do not know whether I can bear to do so.

Then we all went off to church. When they wheeled in the coffin I could not help wondering what had happened to the spirit of that smiling, pretty, worldly old woman. The maids, all in black, sat at the back of the church. When we came out I saw the two of them were sobbing. I think they were the only ones there who really mourned Aunt Zaidée.

When we got back to the house Elizabeth said that there were two cases of "Peninsular War" Madeira, supposed to be a rare and wonderful wine, and that she knew Aunt Zaidée would have wished me to have them, so they will be sent to me at Oxford.

The day of my luncheon with Margot. I was extremely
nervous about the outcome of it. I ordered lobster and
hock and got some flowers for the table. The only ones
they had were uninteresting carnations. The scout arranged them in a tankard of college silver. The first thing
that Margot said when she had taken off her coat was,
"May I, please?" and picked up the tankard to re-
arrange the carnations. Then she walked round the room
peering at the pictures on the walls in a way which I now
see is shortsighted and accounts for her puckering up her
eyes when she looks at you.

I remember nothing of the luncheon-table conversation between us except that she talked away in a sort of
Noel Coward lingo while the poodle lay under the table.
She had insisted on bringing it with her although dogs
are not allowed in college. She smuggled it under her
coat.

After luncheon I suggested a liqueur. "A tiny crème de
menthe," she said. "I am going to tea with Vi and her
mother later and I mustn't come reeling in." We put
down our liqueurs and subsided onto the sofa together.
Her conversation switched off as you would switch off a
light. The transition was complete. It was just the sensation of dancing with someone who by sheer instinct keeps
perfectly in step as if you were listening to the same tune
and our limbs moved of their own accord.

Later when she got up from the sofa she looked at herself in the glass of her compact and said, "Oh, my hair. I
look a fright." The only change was that she did not say
it in her Mayfair accent, and then she said to the poodle,
"Come to mother, my little pooch. Isn't he a good good
dog?", cuddling its nose against her cheek. The poodle
was indeed a good dog. During the whole of our interlude
on the sofa he remained under the table without moving
but far from asleep, watching us with an alert, sophisticated gaze.

I accompanied Margot out of the college. As we went

through the porter's lodge there were Miles and Ducker apparently studying announcements of forthcoming sporting and dramatic events. Ducker's eyes slid sideways at us as we passed and then hastily swivelled back to concentration on the date and time of the Pembroke-versus-Magdalen soccer match. Margot had by now resumed her social manner. "Oh, it would be too ghastly for any words if I am late for tea with Vi. Poor lamb, she is absolutely counting on me to help out with her mother, who can be *but* difficult. She doesn't seem to realize that Vi is a grown woman who has to lead her own life," and then she was gone up St. Aldates on her high heels, dragging the poodle in her wake, and calling out, "Good-bye for now, my sweet. It was a divine lunch. That lobster . . . "

When I got back to my room I lay down on the sofa and gave myself up to non-thinking, almost dozing, when there was a knock on the door. It was Millin, the porter. "Sorry to disturb you, sir, but I thought as your guest has left I might mention there is an American lady and gentleman in the Lodge who are most anxious to see Dr. Johnson's teapot. They have been waiting quite some time but they won't be discouraged." "Millin," I said sleepily, "these rooms are not a museum." "You will recall, sir, that the Dean said that, in reason, guests might come and look about from time to time." I do indeed recall the arrangement; it was the condition for my having these rooms, some of the best in college, so I said to Millin to ask them to come up, that I was just going out anyway. Before I could get down the staircase they were at the door. "I hope this is not an invasion of your pryvacy," the lady said with a brilliant smile. "It must be a real inspiration for you to be in these rooms where he lived and studied." Her husband, a tall, pale man with thick-lensed glasses, had now followed her up the stairs and was gazing about him. "That sofa is a fine piece," he said. "Did it belong to the doctor?" "Oh Buddy," his wife cried, "that is *modern*." I pointed out the teapot which stands by itself in an alcove by the fireplace and turning to me she said, "Can't you just see him brewing himself a pot of tea as he bent over his books. Perhaps we interrupted you just as you were going to make tea yourself out of that very teapot." I said that as a matter of fact I had just been doing a spot of work.

When they had gone I decided to go out. Feeling idiotically happy I walked aimlessly along the Cornmarket thinking of Margot and myself when to my amazement I saw Margot herself emerging from Elliston and Caddell's tea-room arm in arm with Jeremy. I don't think they saw me. I headed for Christ Church Meadows and plumped myself down on a damp wooden bench and I thought, why would Margot spin that story of going to catch a bus to tea with Vi and her mother. I have no claim on her. She has a perfect right to have tea with Jeremy or do anything else she wants. Did she tell me that silly tale for the sheer pleasure of bamboozling me? In any case it doesn't matter, but the question is there.

November 28

I woke up feeling like a million dollars. I have done it. I have brought it off. Nothing can take this away from me, even if I never see Margot again. Before she left I said I would telephone her. She said, "No, don't do that, I'll telephone you." I wonder if she ever will. My body remembers hers all the time. I feel so immensely pleased, as if some weight of doubt had been miraculously lifted. Now, when Patterson, Sarkies, and company are describing their exploits it won't disturb me any more, and I shall keep my mouth shut, because once it has really happened it would spoil it to talk about it.

Jim Patterson took me for a spin in his new racing Amilcar. It is painted scarlet and looks very dashing and he is very proud of it. We went at eighty miles an hour on the road to Broadway. It was exhilarating but bloody cold as there is no windscreen on the car. We were both in high spirits. He because of the car, and I because of Margot. We had cold ham and hock for lunch at the Lygon Arms.

137

On the way back the car engine began to peter out and we had to turn in to a garage and hang about there for what seemed hours while the mechanic peered under the hood and mumbled about carburettors and big-ends. Jim said, "Christ, I hope it isn't the big-end," and I agreed, although to tell the truth I don't know what a big-end is. Finally they got the car so that it was going and we got back to Oxford in the late afternoon just in time for me to go to Germers' for a haircut and a soothing massage from the overhead vibrators, one of the minor pleasures of life, but the barbers don't like them because they say they store up hair and it blows out and makes them cough.

I dined in Hall like a good boy and talked to the Senior Scholar, who is rather depressed as he has been gated for getting drunk and beating on a tin can outside the Dean's window shouting "Ecclesiastical buggery!"

November 29
No call from Margot. Fortunately I have not got her telephone number or I should be tempted to ring her up and I am sure that would be a mistake.

I went for a drink this evening with Leslie Mahon. He is the wittiest little creature I have met here. Sparkling with spirits and fun, but at times he falls into mawkish and querulous moods. Also he paints his face, which doesn't go at all with his blue-black compexion, as he is one of those unfortunates who have to shave twice a day.

He took me to the George for dinner and talked at the top of his voice, saying to me, "Darling, do have some more of this divine pâté." I felt very conspicuous, especially as luck would have it Kenworthy and Martin, who were at prep school with me, were at the next table. They put on boot-button faces and talked in lowered tones, I suppose saying what queer company I had got into. After dinner Leslie said, "Let's go to the Nag's Head and have a drink." The Nag's Head is a pub with a reputation for being frequented by homosexuals and is where they pick

138

up men, but I thought, "What the hell, why not, let's see what it's like."

The moment we got into the pub Leslie, who had been talking very interestingly, became a different person and began putting on coquettish airs and flaunting about the place. There were only half a dozen working men there drinking beer, but they all seemed to know Leslie and treated him tolerantly as if he were a showing-off child. He soon attached himself to one particular youth and I was left to exchange remarks about the weather with two young men at the bar. They treated me with some suspicion as though I was a kind of spy, then the door flew open and a troupe of aesthetes came willowing in waving silk handkerchiefs and cooing and gasping, and soon were entangled with the men in the pub in bantering conversations and sidelong glances.

I went up to Leslie to ask him if he was ready to go home but saw that he was stroking the young workman's cheek and reciting some lines of his play to him, so I bowed out and thought they were all relieved to see the last of me.

November 30
Margot telephoned me this morning and suggested my going round to her house tomorrow evening. So, she must have been thinking of me during these last two days in the same way that I have been thinking of her.

She lives in the Iffley Road and I am to be there about six. I tried to work on my essay but I couldn't settle to anything, so walked up to the Mitre with the intention of having a solitary sausage and mash in the pub part of the hotel and coming back to work, but there I ran into Jim Patterson, who was very down in the mouth. There is something seriously wrong with his beloved Amilcar and he is afraid he has been sold a pup, so we had a couple of whiskies to cheer us up and then decided it was not a good day for work and we might as well go to the movies and just sink into the plush seats at the Super Cinema and relax. There is something delightfully immoral about going to an afternoon movie at Oxford. It is such a supreme waste of time. (I remember Tony in Halifax used to say, "It is a sunny day today, almost fine enough to go to the movies!")

On our way down the High we ran into Betty and that other prostitute who is her hanger-on and picks up the crumbs that fall from Betty's table. On the spur of the moment we asked them to come to the movies with us. It was a risky thing to do, as if the Proctors had seen us with them we would have been in trouble — fined or gated, or both, especially as Betty is so well-known to them. But as the Proctors are not usually around in the middle of the afternoon, we chanced it.

Betty is not at all unattractive with her broad pink country face, but they say she has the clap. Anyway, I wasn't tempted. I am seeing Margot tomorrow.

The movie was *Chicago*, a really amazing film. Phyllis Haver gave a magnificent performance as the baby-faced Chicago murderess. I wonder what was going through the girls' heads while they were watching it. I shouldn't think it would be at all their idea of fun, but they seemed quite pleased to be asked to the movies like ordinary girls with no strings attached, but I'm not sure, as when I asked Betty which she preferred — townees or undergraduates — she said, "Pardon me for saying so, but undergraduates are a bloody silly lot," and she should know.

December 1

I went to see Margot this afternoon. It was a pouring rainy day and she lives miles out in the wastes of the Iffley Road. I had not realized that it would take so long to walk there, and to my horror when I looked at my watch it was six-thirty and still I had not got there. I was in a panic at the idea of being late when all day I had thought of nothing but being with her, and I almost ran the rest of the way.

She lives in a small red-brick house exactly like all the other houses in the street, with a dusty-looking hydrangea outside the door. When you go in there is a coat-rack on the left, much too big for the hall, and on the right the door into the sitting-room, which also is quite small with a heavy Victorian dresser and a shiny horsehair sofa. It is a rented house and Margot said the furniture came with the house.

When I came in she was sitting with the poodle asleep beside her and her feet curled under her close to the gas fire drinking gin. She greeted me pretty coolly. "Surprise, surprise. So you have decided to drop in after all. Now you are here pour yourself a drink and come and sit by the fire. This room is *but* freezing." So I squatted down beside her and she suddenly stopped talking, just the way she did the last time, and was quite silent, as if this was a signal.

Upstairs there is an old-fashioned huge mahogany double bed that practically fills the bedroom. Much later, when I woke from a kind of half doze, the first thing that my eyes lighted on was the picture of a man with a handlebar moustache, wearing some kind of a sola topi, hanging on the wall opposite. This absurd picture made me smile with complete happiness. Margot said, "I am always meaning to take that down. It is such a hideosity." I said, "Leave it there, it brings good luck."

We went downstairs and had bread and cheese and some more gin. Margot began shortening the hem of a dress, sticking pins in it to show how it should go. It was quite a domestic scene. Looking round the room I thought of the stories I had heard of "the notorious Margot Poltimer" and the orgies she was supposed to preside over. I cannot imagine an orgy in the sitting-room, certainly not on the horsehair sofa, and when I looked at Margot sitting on the other side of the gas fire sewing, I wondered how she had got such a reputation. I know she must be fairly promiscuous, otherwise why me? But so are lots of women without being so much talked about.

She doesn't do the talking. She has not mentioned another man to me except to speak of Jeremy rather vaguely as a friend. I expect it is because undergraduates are such gossips, and exaggerate everything as they do, and the men she has slept with boast about it and paint her as a great courtesan to prove that they are cordon bleu lovers. Also, she is a different person in public — puts on an act the way she did when I met her in the George bar. (That was only a week ago and I feel as though I have known her much longer.) One odd thing about her, she hates to be asked questions. When I said, "What are you doing next week?" she flashed right back, "Mind your own business my sweet." All the same, she said she would have dinner with me on Thursday.

December 2
Before I was properly awake I was picturing Margot lying beside me. I jumped out of bed saying to myself, "I'll go mad if I go on like this," and so I dressed in a hurry without taking time to shave and went for a walk in Christ Church Meadows. I looked across the field at Merton College half enshrouded in damp mist and had an extraordinarily intense vision of the beauty of the scene. It was almost as physical as the feeling I had had a few moments before when I was picturing Margot's body. I walked till I was tired and hungry and went back to my room and ate an enormous breakfast of kidneys and bacon.

I worked all day until five o'clock without stopping for lunch and then Matza and Jeremy dropped in and I went with them to the billiard saloon. By this time it was raining hard. I stood around watching them play for a little, then I collapsed on a sofa in front of an enormous coal fire and dozed off to the sounds of the clicking billiard balls and the rain on the window panes and the coals shifting in the fire.

December 3

Today Jeremy motored me over to the du Plat Taylors' for lunch. They have left Newfoundland and now live only an hour or so from here in a village in Buckinghamshire. Their house is a pretty Georgian ex-rectory. They have invited me there several times, but this time they said that Eric Smith would be there, which was a great added inducement. They gave me a warm welcome, but the house was bloody cold, even for an English house in the country, so I see they have not lost their liking for discomfort which they enjoyed so much in Newfoundland.

Mrs. du Plat Taylor has not changed a bit — as majestic as ever. The Colonel looks much older and rather shaky. He still has that appalling set of false teeth. Cynthia works at the neighbouring kennels. She always wanted to do that. She seemed glad to see me again, in her undemonstrative fashion. Eric Smith was as delightful as ever and very friendly to me, but he has got thicker somehow. Not fatter, but thicker and almost middle-aged-looking. He had driven over from a neighbouring country house with a dark-eyed rather silent woman. I thought he seemed pretty keen about her. I only had a chance to talk to him alone for a few moments when we took a turn in the garden together, and he went on just as he used to do about his plans and projects for the future. It is always the future with him. There was only one awkward moment when I tactlessly asked him how he was getting on with Iris, the "unwieldy woman" whom he had confided to me at Black Duck he intended to marry. He looked quite surprised and not at all pleased and said, "How did you know about her? Anyway, it is all washed up ages ago." He had obviously forgotten ever telling me about her. When I left he said I must look him up the next time I was in town, but I am not sure that he meant it.

It was rather strange seeing the du Plat Taylors and Eric in a different setting, and somehow disappointing. They did not seem as exceptional as they seemed to me in

Newfoundland. More like other people. Perhaps it is because I am older. Jeremy was on his best behaviour at lunch and quite charmed the du Plat Taylors. He was really rather bored by the whole thing.

December 4

Thinking about the other night's visit to the Nag's Head. A sort of mist of homosexuality does hang over Oxford like the mist of the Thames Valley and it would be hard to imagine the place without it. It is not so much actual buggery, though doubtless there is some of that too, it is more a matter of teasing attractions and rebuffs and friendships mixed with attraction and tinged with sentiment. But isn't all friendship mixed with attraction and tinged with sentiment? Mine certainly is.

In the morning I went to Professor Baker's lecture on Economics. He is one of the better lecturers and to my surprise I find the subject interesting. Most of the economic and monetary theory is over my head and I never had much head for theory of any kind, but the practical side of it — the levels of wages, the social conditions, and the role of the unions — is quite engrossing. Also, social history is beginning to interest me. The economic side of the Crusades and the Expropriation of the Monasteries and the Land Enclosures in the eighteenth century. I was very ignorant of all these. Most of the history I have read has dealt with treaties, wars, dynasties, alliances, and personalities, and so was very one-sided.

While I was working Anstruther-Gray came in. He says Oxford is a waste of time and has decided to join the police in West Africa. This is good news, but God help the natives with this bullying braggart in charge of them. He is the kind of Englishman who "gives the Empire a bad name" as Mother would say. However, he began to talk about his own upbringing at home. How his father used to beat him up unmercifully to "make a man of him", and how terrified he was of him. This explains a lot about Anstruther-Gray, but not enough to make him tolerable.

In the evening I had tea with the Master and Mrs. Homes-Dudden. They ask each member of the college to tea once a year. It is like a royal audience. The Master is magnificent — the handsomest man in Oxford and very genial in the grand manner. Mrs. Homes-Dudden is a thin, tall, yellow-faced woman with a sharp tongue and a critical eye. She is said to be kinder than she seems, which would not be difficult.

We had tea in their big high-ceilinged drawing-room. Acres of nondescript carpet, some fine china, and a blazing hot fire. The Master showed me a pretty little table that the Queen gave him as a souvenir of his preaching at Sandringham. I should not be surprised if he ended up as an archbishop.

December 5
I woke up to a surprise this morning. It had snowed overnight. I have never seen Oxford under snow before. The Quads look like white linen handkerchiefs. I must say I am delighted to be at Pembroke College. It was good luck for me coming here. The place has an atmosphere of its own. I suppose all the colleges have, but Pembroke has something friendly and informal about it and I wouldn't be at any other college. It is, I am afraid, at rather a low ebb in its fortunes, not at all in the lead academically or in athletics. The undergraduates are a curious mixture. A small group of Scholars, several from the Channel Islands, which have some special connection with Pembroke; a smattering of rather gilded foreigners; some Paris Americans; a brace or two of Rhodes Scholars; some raffish men from the grander public schools who failed to get into other colleges; and a sub-stratum of ordinary chaps from ordinary schools — all presided over by the Master, who billows through the Quads in his ample gown like Jupiter descending from the clouds.

In the evening went with Jim Patterson to the Super Cinema — Adolphe Menjou in *Surrender* — a slight but charming film. Jim says there is a rumour of having talking films at the Super to replace the silent ones. I intend to start a protest group. Talking films would absolutely ruin the movies.

Jim came back to my rooms and we sat up for hours. He is determined on an adventurous life and thinks none other is worth having, and I daresay he will have one. He has the nerve for it. I find him not as attractive as Jeremy, but a good friend.

Aunt Zaidée's case of Peninsular War Madeira has arrived from Cheltenham and I am planning to have a dinner party in my rooms to celebrate the event.

December 6
Tonight was to have been the night of my dinner with Margot but she telephoned this morning with some long tale of Vi's mother being ill and Vi didn't like to leave her alone, *but* she had promised to have dinner tonight with Cedric Anstruther-Gray, so Margot had said she would go and spend the evening with Vi's mother and she had the nerve to say that she knew I would not mind! It is maddening, all the more so because my evening with Margot is to be sacrificed to the insufferable Anstruther-Gray. She says she will have dinner with me tomorrow.

I tried to settle down to writing my essay on the topic "The eighteenth century marked the low watermark of international morality", and I think my bad temper and frustration at being put off by Margot actually helped me to demolish this absurd proposition and to build up the case for the twentieth century being "the low watermark". However, as there is no such thing as "international morality" it doesn't really matter which century you pick on.

In the afternoon I ran into Jeremy and Jim in the High. We all went back to Jeremy's rooms, where we were joined by a noisy but nice Harrovian. We practised shooting a revolver at an egg cup. Jim hit it every single time — I not once.

Came home and read Barbellion's *Diary of a Disap-*

pointed Man and could not face going into Hall, so went to sleep in front of the fire and when I woke up at two a.m. the fire had gone out and the room was as cold as an ice-box.

December 7

I had lunch to-day with precious Branksome of Eton and Magdalen, who looks like a suave, rather supercilious shop-walker with his hair parted in the middle. There were quite long pauses in the conversation during which he occasionally lowered a remark into the silences, such as "modern poetry has outgrown the investing of local patriotism with aesthetic significance." What was my astonishment when, as we were walking out of the porter's lodge of Magdalen, he asked me if I knew "a really remarkable young woman called Margot Poltimer". It seemed such an extraordinary coincidence that I wondered if he had the power of reading other people's thoughts. Also, I cannot imagine what he and she could have in common, but he said, airily, "she is a charming creature, don't you think? As a matter of fact I am having tea with her to-day."

When I got to Margot's this evening to take her out to dinner, the first thing I asked her was whether she knew Branksome, and she said, "Oh yes, he dropped in unexpectedly to-day. Too, *too* tiresome." I did not pursue the subject, but now I am convinced that she must see him fairly often and has mentioned my name to him, so that he only asked me to lunch to score off me by showing me that he had been there first. Anyway, it is none of my business who she sees or how often.

I wanted to take her to dinner at the George but she said, "Oh, that is so expensive, don't waste your money. I hate waste. Let's go somewhere cheaper." (So much for the legend that she is a gold-digger.) So we went to the Candied Friend, where we had a most insipid dinner of fillet of plaice, finishing off with *apple surprise*, which is just apple sauce, in a room hung with "The Cries of

London", waited on by waitresses in mob-caps. The tables were so close together that we could not really talk to each other, but she did look so lovely in that dreary restaurant I was proud to be seen with her. She wore a black dress which made her fairness seem quite startling.

When we got back to the Iffley Road she was very sweet, even affectionate, which she has never been before.

December 8

In the morning read Aristotle's *Politics*. I like this — "to be always seeking after the useful does not become free and exalted souls." In the afternoon I went to an exhibition of modern paintings at Ryman's. One of the pictures by a new artist called Christopher Wood I liked very much, then to the Super with Jeremy to see Harold Lloyd in *For Heaven's Sake*. He is the funniest comedian of all. Far funnier to me than Charlie Chaplin. In the evening I dined with Jackson and Clere Parsons and some of their friends. The conversation was out of my range. A rapid crossfire exchange about modern literature, music, and painting. When I find myself in a group of really cultured people I am uncomfortably aware of my own ignorance. When I am with the little set of Jeremy, Anstruther-Gray, etc., I can delude myself that I am almost a civilized man, and so I am in comparison to them. The worst of it is that I have gone backwards since I came to Oxford. I seem to have reverted to the mentality of an irresponsible schoolboy without intellectual curiosity. Also the poetry, criticism, etc., which I read at home is looked on here as hopelessly out of date. For instance, Lawrence Binyon, Maurice Baring, Lascelles Abercrombie, and Blunden. As for Rupert Brooke, they say he is "for schoolgirls", and the literary critics I followed like Edmund Gosse and Saintsbury are not taken seriously.

December 9

I met Leslie Mahon at the Super for coffee this morning. The place was packed as usual so that you can hardly thread your way through the extra tables and chairs they bring in to pick up the extra custom. It really is a peculiar institution. Why do we all crowd in to that place, blue with smoke, noisy with chatter, to sit on hard chairs at tiny, rickety tables and drink cups of tepid coffee and nibble damp chocolate biscuits? Leslie and I were put in a corner, which I was quite glad of, as I still feel conspicuous being seen with him. If only he would not wear a silk handkerchief clasped by a bracelet to his wrist and wave at his acquaintances with it.

He was in a very nervous mood to-day, and when the waiter spilt some coffee over his shoulder he said, "This is *too* much. We must escape from this stinking badgers' den." When we got out and were walking down the street he said, "I must tell you the most awful thing has happened. Last night I had drink taken and thought I would just pop in for a minute to see Roger. He was alone, sitting by the fire and looking so divine with the firelight on his golden hair, so perfect and so ruddy. He asked me to sit beside him on the sofa and we talked as we have never talked before. It was the most perfect time we have ever had together. Then I spoilt it all. I suddenly heard myself saying, 'I love you'. He just got up from the sofa and stood in front of the fire, his poor face was *pink* with embarrassment, then he said in a sort of strangled way, 'I am sorry'. That was all he said, but it was death to me. I shall never be able to look him in the face again. I didn't close my eyes all last night, and then a shattering idea occurred to me in the small hours of the morning. My dear, what do you think it was? I thought that if I had made a real pass at him it might have been all right. It was those fatal words 'I love you', and the agony is that I do."

Poor Leslie. I felt so sorry for him.

December 10
What a drama! This is what happened, so far as I can remember it. Last night was my dinner party to celebrate the Peninsular War Madeira. I wanted it to be regardless

of expense so I ordered lobsters and venison. The electric lights were put out and the scout borrowed some college silver candelabra so that the candle-light glimmered appropriately against the panelling of the room, a perfect setting.

I had asked Jeremy, Jim Patterson, Anstruther-Gray, Matza, and Sarkies. I have never been a host like this before. All came in dinner jackets. At first we stood about feeling rather self-conscious, but relaxed with the drinks; then, at the close of dinner, came the great moment of pouring the ancient wine. Jeremy got up and made a speech, saying how sporting I had been to share this wine, which was the same that the great Wellington had drunk, and commiserating with me on my bad luck at cards this term, which was bloody nice of him. Then I thought I saw a queer look on the faces of the others as they drank the Madeira, and I took a sip myself. It was like clotted vinegar, and there was the whole case of it. Jeremy pretended that it was not too bad and said we were just not used to wine of that age, but it was no good. No-one could force it down, and there was no other wine left. Nothing but a couple of bottles of gin. I think it was the gin that did it.

The scout had cleared the table away and we were setting up a table for roulette when someone produced a pistol and started taking shots at the lamp in the street. One or two others went to the window and joined him in the shooting. There was a lot of laughing and shouting. I was standing at the window watching when I saw two passers-by going under the lamp-post, a man and a girl, and to my horror as a shot was fired I saw the girl stumble and collapse on the pavement. I shall never forget that moment. The man called up at us, "Get a doctor. She has been hit." So Jeremy and I ran across the Quad to telephone for a doctor.

As we were trying to get through on the telephone, who should emerge in the Lodge but the Dean. He said, in a very cutting voice, that he was at a loss to understand the unseemly noise at this hour coming from my rooms and he fancied he had heard shots fired, so of course we had to explain what had happened, pointing out that it had been only a Rag. He said, "I doubt if it will be so regarded," and swept up to my rooms, giving one look around at the guests, who were pretty white and shaken, and said, "Gentlemen, go to your rooms at once and do not leave them until you receive further instructions. This is a most disgraceful affair. You should all be ashamed, both for yourselves and the discredit you have brought on the college. What the condition of the unfortunate victim of your behaviour is we do not know, but for your sakes I hope it is not serious." Jeremy then said that he had seen the woman get up from the pavement and go limping along the street leaning on the arm of the man, so that the injury could not be too bad. "That is as may be," said the Dean.

About an hour later the doctor whom we had telephoned called through to the porter's lodge to say that the injured woman had had two pellets extracted from the fleshy part of her leg and that she is "resting comfortably at her home". So far so good.

December 11
We all met at the Super this morning (except Matza, who had shut himself up in his rooms and said he would see no-one) and talked over the shooting and its consequences. Of course, news of it has spread and we find ourselves rather celebrities. Some of our acquaintances enjoy prophesying the most dire consequences for us, that we shall end up in Wormwood Scrubbs, disowned by our families, or have to emigrate to the colonies. Someone said "to Canada". So I said, "That would suit me as I come from there anyway, and moreover, Canada does not happen to be a colony." They said, "What's the difference? It's part of the Empire isn't it?" That is all they know about Canada.

It is funny the way this shooting affair shows up

people's characters. Jeremy is cool and easy, making a joke of the whole thing. Anstruther-Gray boasts for one moment that he fired the fatal shot, and the next moment tries to put the blame on me for giving the party in the first place. Sarkies, as a third-year man, is the most likely to be held responsible and to be sent down from Oxford, but he does not seem to give a damn. The most peculiar behaviour is that of Matza. When he did not turn up at the Super I went round to his rooms. He was in a terrible state of funk. He had had the door bolted and his man-servant stationed on the stairs to warn him if the police were coming, so that he could make good his escape by the back passage. He seems to imagine that he will be consigned to an *oubliette*, also he is determined never to see any members of the "little set" again, as he finds them "in very bad taste", which is rather much coming from an Egyptian! He said that if it came to a court case his picture might be in the Cairo newspapers and what would his uncles and aunts say. I was rather nettled by this and said my picture might be in the Nova Scotian papers and what would *my* aunts say, but he did not seem to think that that would be at all the same thing.

December 12

In the morning Jeremy and I went to consult a lawyer. He says the woman will probably bring damages against us in the Civil Court as well as the case coming before the Proctors. Most unfortunately for us it turns out that she is one of the secretaries in the office of the Mayor of Oxford, and the Mayor is quite annoyed about the whole business and threatens to make a fuss.

This morning when I opened the London newspaper there was a leading article about our case which said that a group of undergraduates of "the idle rich class" had been amusing themselves by sitting at a window of their rooms in an "exclusive" college taking pot-shots at the honest citizenry of Oxford and had stricken down an in-nocent girl as she walked by her sweetheart's side. The article extended sympathy to her sorrowing family and expressed horror at the deed which reminded the writer of the excesses of Rome in its decadence. He hoped that the perpetrators of the crime would be condignly punished and made an example of. How did they get hold of the story? Perhaps the Mayor of Oxford put them up to it as there was another quite disagreeable article on the same lines in the *Oxford Times*.

Of course it is all part of the current press campaign about the wickedness and degeneracy of the young, and how we have no moral standards.

In the evening we went in a group — Jeremy, Anstruther-Gray, Jim Patterson and I — to apologize to the girl at her family's house. When we got there they were all posed as though for a group photograph. The girl sitting in a chair with her leg up on a footstool. Her father and mother and brother ranged behind her and the young man who had been with her when it happened standing beside her looking very sheepish. They stood about her chair as if to protect her from further assault. Jeremy put out all his charm and I was tremendously sympathetic. Anstruther-Gray was as tactless as usual. However, it did not make much difference, as I could see that they are determined to press the matter just as hard as they can and get every last cent out of us.

The girl is not bad-looking, but has a stubborn little receding chin which bodes no good for her young man. Her brother I believe is the real inspirer of her case, spouting a whole lot of legal terms he has got from their lawyer. So we retired no better off than when we came in. The doctor says the injury to her leg has already quite healed up; still I suppose it was a shock to her at the moment and promises profit in the future.

December 13

I have not seen Margot since the shooting affray, and when I went there last night she seemed unusually depressed and said she was sick of Oxford and of her life

153

here and longed to get away for a change, and then she suddenly said, "Charles, why don't we go to Paris together when university vacation begins? I have always craved to see Paris, and it would be so divine to be there together. I can just picture the two of us sitting in one of those cafés in the Champs-Elysées. The only thing is that poor you would have to pay for most of it. I might just have enough for my return fare, but nothing over. My bloody husband has reduced my allowance again."

We went on talking about Paris, getting very excited at the prospect. All the time I knew it was impossible. I am overdrawn already at the bank, apart from my debts, and in cash I have less than eighteen pounds to last me for the entire vacation, but I pretended to believe in our going to Paris. Perhaps she was only pretending too. I do not know. But we seemed closer together than ever before.

As I was getting up to leave, I saw on the table by the bed a tortoise-shell cigarette case which is the one that I gave Jeremy to show my gratitude for his staking my losses at vingt-et-un. He must have left it there one time when he was leaving.

As I walked home I thought that Margot's sadness and discontent tonight, and her wanting to go to Paris with me, have made me feel that I could love her, but I know that that would be a big mistake. The term is nearly over and we shall all be going down in a few days.

December 14

To-day I had a final tutorial. My tutor says that my essays are lucidly and interestingly written, but do not represent "any cataclysmic energy on my part" and seem to skate over the surface rather than plumb the depths. "Cataclysmic energy" indeed! "Plumbing the depths"! Well I devoted this morning to "plumbing the depths" of my finances. Apart from the impending Battels bill, I owe Jeremy £47 for unpaid gambling debts, and Shepherd the tailor £32 for those two lousy ill-fitting suits, not to mention other smaller debts.

I was rather consoled by Jim Patterson coming in and laughing at my debts as a joke compared with his. Now, not content with the ill-fated Amilcar, he is proposing to buy a horse and compete in the University Steeple Chase, despite the fact that the one time I rode with him in Folly Meadow I could see that William, at home, would not have allowed him to take out one of the livery-stable horses.

I wonder where the notion of "carefree under-graduates", as described for instance by E .F. Benson in his novels, ever came from. Most of my friends are hag-ridden by debts; dreading exams; and sexually frustrated in one way or another. Yet who would want to be anywhere but at Oxford? Certainly not I.

December 15
Sunday afternoon in Oxford on a damp, dark day in December. Oh the charnel gloom of it. The feeling that nothing will ever happen again. The ivy climbing on an iron gate outside a red-brick North Oxford villa makes you turn your eyes away.

I went into the musty, empty Union to write a letter to Mother, and could think of nothing to say to her that would not be a lie. She has an idea of my Oxford life that I used to have before I came up here — that I am taking advantage of a wonderful opportunity for which she is making sacrifices, and how can I explain to her what is really happening to me, especially as I don't understand it myself. Perhaps it is a sort of education, but not what we planned.

After writing a very dull letter I had some tea and cinnamon toast and wandered into the library, picking one book after another out of the shelves, but I could not settle to any one. It is said that T. E. Lawrence, when he was at Oxford, read every book in the Oxford Library. I began to calculate how many hours this would have taken him and it works out as a mathematical impossibility, unless he had done nothing but read, never sleeping or eating and reading three books an hour. Then I thought, why don't I drop in and see Margot. I know she does not like me to come in on Sundays, but I thought I would chance it, so I did.

When I got there I found her and Vi lying on the bed upstairs smoking cigarettes with their shoes off. They had just been at a luncheon party and were talking about the men there, comparing notes about their admirers and giggling together. I sat on a chair at the foot of the bed and they paid no attention to me. Vi said that Anstruther-Gray thought he was a great lover, but that that was a "big joke", although he was "rather sweet". Considering that Anstruther-Gray thinks that Vi dotes on him, this surprised me considerably. I felt that I was listening to the secrets of the Seraglio and I wondered when it would be my turn to be discussed as though I was not there.

Then they got into a discussion about a hat of Margot's that she was going to sell to Vi. "Well then, fifteen shillings it is," said Margot. "But you said twelve and six before," said Vi. "No, my dear, you must have misunderstood me. It was always fifteen shillings." "Yesterday you did say twelve and six." They went on and on like this till I went downstairs to the sitting-room and read the Sunday papers.

Later on Margot came down and said, "I have been trying to get rid of Vi but she simply won't go." So I took the hint and left myself.

It has been a very unsuccessful Sunday.

December 16
The last day of term. Our case is now out of the Proctor's hands and will come up in Court at the beginning of next term. The college has been surprisingly indulgent about it, and we have been let off with a warning. I shall be on my way to London tomorrow to spend Christmas with my cousins, the Adlingtons. They say the elder daughter, Mary, is a great beauty and I am anxious to meet her.

January 15, 1927

I gave up writing this diary during the vacation. I decided that it is unhealthy because it encourages me to see my life as a looker-on; also it is a waste of time when I should be working. I did do quite a lot of work, among other things, during the vacation, but now I find it impossible to resist returning to the diary. I know it is a bad habit, like smoking or drinking, but I cannot give it up any longer.

To-day was a blustery, dusty day. I woke up full of new resolutions. This term is going to be very different from last term. One difference will be that I am going to work five hours a day regularly. McCallum says that if I do this I might even get a First, but I doubt it. Secondly, I am going to take regular exercise. I have been seeing more of Wynne Paton, and he has convinced me that half my depressions and bad moods are due to lack of exercise. I am going to continue boxing with Paton three times a week and we are also going out with the Christ Church Beagles. My third, and most important resolution is that Anstruther-Gray shall never darken my door again.

In fact, the "little set" is breaking up. We saw too much of each other under the strain of the shooting affray, and boredom has set in. I have not seen Margot yet. She has been on a visit to her husband in London. Jeremy tells me that during the vacation she was seeing a lot of that fellow Frankie Turner, the man I saw her with the first time I met her in the George bar. He is an Oxford townee who has a job at the Morris Cowley Works. Apparently Margot has known him since they were children and at one time was engaged to him.

January 16

To-day I went with Paton to the Meet of the Christ Church Beagles at a village near Cowley. We met at Canterbury Gate and went out by bus. It was a still day with a pale blue sky, very cold if you stood still, but we were off ploughing through oceans of mud and scrambling through hedges. It is a peculiar sport as the hare runs in circles, and, when following, one is always coming back to the place one started from. It is like Alice in Wonderland when Alice had to keep running to be where she was at the beginning. At intervals the hounds swerve round and the whole field reverses and instead of being at the rear one finds oneself leading the hunt.

When it was over we all came back to a farm-house for an enormous tea with muffins and cherry jam before a roaring fire. It was great fun but exorbitantly expensive at three shillings each for tea.

January 17
I took Matza to lunch at the George to-day to pay him back for some of his lavish hospitality. At the end of lunch he said, "You know, you should always fold the bill over the tip." I suppose it is good for me to learn these things, but all the same I thought it was rather patronizing.

January 18
I tried to apply myself this morning to Hobbes' *Leviathan*, then I went out to do some shopping and spent about three hours and only bought one pair of shoe-laces. On the way back I stepped on an imitation bird which was hopping on the pavement, and broke it, and had to pay the hawker for it, "if I was a gentleman," he said. I don't feel at all like a gentleman to-day. Then I paid my college Battels bills, which were a third more than I had counted on. I am sure this college must have a crooked accountant.

In the afternoon I went to see Margot, who was back from London. She was friendly but different. She would not let me touch her, and put me off with a kind of steely indifference.

In the evening I came back to write my essay on "The Formation of Parties under Charles II", but I couldn't get on with it and paced about my room in a bad temper, knocked over the lamp by my bed and broke it.

January 19
Went to a very funny comedy, Louise Fazenda was in it, and then went to tea with Jackson and got into an argument about religion. He said, "Surely as an intellectual you can't say that." I said, "But I am not an intellectual." He said, "If you are not an intellectual, what are you?" It's a good question and I don't know the answer.

January 20
Margot had a party to-day. She has been talking about this project for some time, saying that she should do something to cheer up Vi's mother, who has been very depressed and has been complaining that after all she has done for Vi, she is now cast aside like an old shoe. I was quite curious to see Vi's mother. I had almost begun to doubt her existence, as Margot makes her the excuse for every last-minute postponement of our meetings. Well, she does exist, although quite different from the ill-used, pathetic old lady I had pictured.

She arrived at the party before the others and turned out to be a bosomy Thames Valley ex-blonde in her forties who downed a couple of gins — she said it was to cheer her up as she had been "feeling worse than death with worry over Vi". (I wondered if Margot has picked up her phoney Mayfair way of talking from this old girl.) Vi's mother backed me into a corner and, although I was meeting her for the first time, began a long tarradiddle about how sad it was that Vi lacked appeal for men. "Of course she has Cedric hanging about, but if you ask me I don't think he is serious. I mean, she is twenty-seven and has never had what I call a *real* proposal yet. It is so hard for me to understand as I was married to her father out of the schoolroom when I was sixteen and I have had men after me all my life. Of course Vi has the brains. But that is not the same thing, is it?" (I am certainly surprised to hear about Vi's brains, as she has always struck me as being very nearly half-witted.)

While she was going on like this, that man Frankie Turner came in. He has a disgustingly curly mouth and curly black hair. Margot greeted this individual as a long-lost friend. "Darling, would you see to the drinks." So, he went over to the side table and began by helping himself to a mahogany-coloured whisky, saying to Margot, "Where the hell are the big glasses?", as if he was entirely at home in the house. Then the room began to fill up. No more women, but Jeremy with a hangover, and Jim Patterson and some assorted undergraduates, including that man Branksome from Magdalen. Then Anstruther-Gray appeared with a stout, squat, bearded man wearing an Arab head-dress, introduced as the Emir of Zkwat, and an unshaven Scotsman with pink eyelashes who, according to Anstruther-Gray, is "the greatest philosopher Balliol has ever produced". He also said the Emir "owned half Arabia". Vi's mother attached herself to him and I heard her say, "I have always longed to visit the desert. It must be so divinely empty." The Emir gave something between a grunt and a belch. He drank only water, but McAvity the philosopher got into the whisky at once. When I asked him what brand of philosophy he professed, he replied, in a rancid Glasgow accent, "Let me clarrify your thinking, philosophy has no brrands."

By this time someone had turned on the gramophone. Frankie Turner and Margot had gone into the pantry together and were giggling. As the gramophone was playing a tango, Vi's mother swept into the middle of the floor and catching Branksome by both hands said, "Come on, I know you have rhythm. I can always feel these things." He was too feeble to resist, and she began swaying him backwards and forwards to the tune as if he was a rag doll, saying, "No, no — slower darling — that's better — now you've got it." But he hadn't, and she had to give up.

The party went on for hours and everybody, including myself, had a great deal to drink. I don't remember much about the last stages except that Vi's mother, looking very dishevelled, hissed in my ear, "Darling, would you come into the loo with me and help me fish my comb out of the W.C. It has fallen in and I can't get at it." But Vi overheard her and grabbed her by the arm and bundled her off to a taxi.

I stayed on and on hoping to spend the evening with Margot, but Frankie Turner stayed too, and finally Margot said she was going out to dinner with him, so I departed.

January 21
Peter came over for a day and night from Cambridge. We had been planning this reunion for a long time and I am to go to Cambridge to visit him later. He arrived in high spirits and his tales of life at Cambridge make it sound much more exciting than mine at Oxford. He has become passionately interested in the theatre, acts in the Dramatic Society, and wants to have a theatrical career.

We had lunch together and walked in Christ Church Meadows. It seemed as though nothing had changed and we might have been walking together in the park at home. I wanted to take him to Margot's for a drink, but that bloody Frankie Turner was there. I invited Leslie Mahon to join us at the George for dinner, as I thought he would amuse Peter, and they share an interest in the theatre, but it was not a great success, and their talk was rather competitive. After dinner I walked back to the Clarendon Hotel with Peter, where he was staying, and he was very appreciative and nice, so perhaps his visit was not a failure after all.

January 22
I went to a party at St. John's. About forty men were there, all very drunk. I knew no-one except my host and one dreary man who stuck to me like glue. Two chaps

did an exhibition of dancing the Charleston in their dressing-gowns, then two Hungarian barons — famous international homosexuals who were visiting Oxford — joined the party and began dancing with the undergraduates. I had a lot of mixed drinks and they began playing Hawaiian music on the gramophone. For some reason Hawaiian music makes me want to throw up, and the combination with the drinks made me feel quite sick, so I went home and read *Dusty Answer* by Rosamond Lehmann, a new novel about lesbians and homosexuals at Cambridge, which Jackson has lent me.

My cousins the Ponsonbys are coming to live in Oxford. This is great news for me as I started to fall in love with the beautiful daughter Doris when she was visiting Halifax, although she did not give me much encouragement at the time.

January 23

To-day finally our shooting case came up before the magistrate. Only those who had fired the pistol were charged, and as I was not called as a witness I just sat there in the courtroom watching the proceedings, which were soon over. The magistrate gave a lecture and a warning and exacted a pretty heavy fine, so we shall all have to chip in to find the money.

Tomorrow the long-planned motor-race to London takes place. Jeremy, Anstruther-Gray, and Jim Patterson. I am going as Jim's passenger in the Amilcar.

January 24

The day of the race. We all met at the George bar for drinks before the race. Margot and Vi joined us. Margot was accompanied by a short man with a rather wooden face and a dark-brown moustache who remained almost completely silent while the rest of us were celebrating. I asked Jeremy who he was and he said, "Oh, don't you know Brian Poltimer, Margot's husband, he is here on a visit from London." It must have been his voice that an-

swered the telephone the other day when I rang her up as
he said that she was resting and couldn't come to the telephone. She was in fine fettle to-day, greeted me with a
hug and kiss, then tried on Jeremy's crash helmet, which
looked very dashing on her. Vi copied her by putting on
Anstruther-Gray's helmet, which completely submerged
her pin-sized head.

The start of the race was at Magdalen Bridge and off
we sped with our Amilcar in the lead sweeping through
Dorchester, coming round street corners at 40 m.p.h. Jim
was just saying what the disconsolate faces of the others
would be like when they came limping after us to the
rendezvous at the Ritz in London when I heard an omi-
nously familiar sound from the engine. Jim said, "Christ,
it can't be the bloody big-end again," but it was, and the
car slowly conked out and we had to be hauled into a garage in Benson and take the bus back to Oxford in a
pretty sour mood. In the evening there seemed nothing
left to do but to get drunk, so we had dinner at the
George and drank a lot of Asti Spumante and afterwards
went to the Pembroke Smoker and drank innumerable
whiskies with a nameless Rugger Hearty, a silent, good-
looking hulk from Manchester.

January 25
I woke up and took my appalling hangover for a walk
with me through Christ Church Meadows. It must have
been that revolting Asti Spumante. I tottered across the
Quad to see Jim, to hear from him that Jeremy's car
overturned on the way back from London last night. Jeremy is in the Radcliffe Infirmary and will be on his back
for three months with compound fractures of the groin.
He was propped up on the pillows, very talkative and I
think feverish. He was much agitated about money. He
says he owes to half the shops in Oxford, that his mother
has already stumped up £100 to pay his creditors, but
that he had lost it all gambling. He asked me whether I
would go to all his friends and ask them to lend £10 each

and also would arrange to sell the things in his rooms and his car.

I had a most harassing day trying to settle Jeremy's affairs. It should be easy enough to raise £10 each from Jeremy's friends, especially since he has always been so hospitable and generous, but the trouble is that most of them are broke themselves, and Matza, who could easily settle the whole thing, is away in Cairo. Morton, who is supposed to be a friend of Jeremy's, infuriated me to-day by saying that his father had told him that before lending any money he must make it a rule to have a signed i.o.u. — there is a petty tradesman mentality for you! As for selling the contents of Jeremy's rooms — there are all sorts of expensive gadgets, such as a pair of drums for a Jazz Band, brand new gramophone, and gleaming new motor bike, etc., but I doubt if any of these have been paid for, so I hesitate to sell them. Jeremy is too ill to understand the difficulties and is quite impatient. I shall be glad to get away from Oxford for a few days as, to my surprise, Basil Templeton, whom I do not know at all well, has asked me to go to stay with his people in Yorkshire for the local hunt ball and I leave tomorrow.

Basil is at Christ Church. I met him at a party at the end of last term and we struck up a pretty alcoholic friendship.

January 28
To-day I went and bought myself a first-class ticket, although it is an awful waste of money. I was glad I had, because the only other person in the first-class carriage was an extremely attractive girl. We soon began chatting and it turned out that she too was going to Mitcham for the weekend. Her name is Felicity Travers. She had been to stay at Mitcham before. When I asked her what it would be like, she said in a blasé drawl, "Oh, the usual form, you know. The ball will go on forever with a lot of

drunks in pink coats galloping about the floor, stepping on one's feet." I asked her about Basil's family. She said, "There's a widowed mama, not a bad old thing but said by some to be a secret drinker, and Lionel, the younger brother, and of course Basil himself — very much the lord of the manor. Thinks he's God's gift to women, and of course the niece, Muriel. You're asked for her, I imagine. She has been out for simply years but hasn't nabbed a husband, though not for lack of trying. She even went out with the Fishing Fleet to Malta last year and nearly caught someone, but he got off the hook at the last moment." I did not know what the Fishing Fleet meant but she explained that the girls who had missed out in London are sent off to the Mediterranean to see if they can catch a sailor pining for England, Home, and Beauty. Felicity and I seemed to be getting on swimmingly and she said, "I rely on your support if the weekend proves too utterly drear. We can always go for a country ramble together and compare notes."

Muriel, the niece, met us at the station. She is a big girl, not fat but large, with large, handsome features and outsize dark eyes, not bad looking but a bit overpowering. We piled into the family Rolls and drove up to this house which is colonnaded like a Greek temple and is the colour of pale butter. Basil and his brother, Lionel, met us in the hall. He was very welcoming. Then we were shown up to our rooms. Mine looks onto the stables, which are like a barrack square. When we came down to dinner Mrs. Templeton, Basil's mother, greeted me most effusively, saying, "How is dear Canada? I haven't been there since I stayed at Government House in Ottawa. It seems centuries ago." It is quite a hard question to answer, "How is dear Canada?", so I let it slide.

She must have been a real beauty once. In fact you can see from the portrait of her in the hall what she looked like. She is painted coming in from a walk with two setters running beside her and the wind in her hair. She has a vague manner but she certainly doesn't seem like a secret drinker.

The day seemed rather long. Basil took me round the stables, where he has six hunters. He asked me if I hunted and I said, "Good God, no." This made him laugh and he put his arm round my shoulders. I see what Felicity means. He does think he is the lord of all he surveys and so he is, with a property of thousands of acres, an adoring mother, and servants who scurry about at his commands. His brother, Lionel, is a charming, rather shadowy creature with prune-coloured eyes and a curling dark lock falling over his forehead. He knows all about the china and furniture in the house, which Basil takes no interest in except for the interest of possession. What surprises me is that Felicity, after saying that she thought Basil so insufferably conceited, never takes her eyes off him, praises everything he says, and laughs at his very unfunny jokes. Today I was paired off with Muriel and we went for a long walk together across some very damp meadows, scrambling through hedges and over stiles, which she did with great agility. When I put out my hand to help her, quite unnecessarily, over a stile she gave me quite a squeeze. She asked me a lot about Canada and said she supposed that our estates there must be much bigger than theirs in England as the country was so much larger.

After that we all went up to dress for the ball. It is the first time that I have ever worn tails. When I went to tie my white tie I found that it was too short to make a bow. I tried again and again till I was in despair and sat down on the chair saying to myself, "All right, I can't go to the bloody ball at all and I'll send down a message to say I have been taken ill." Then it occurred to me that I could borrow a tie from someone, so I rang the bell and the butler appeared in person. He looked at my tie and said he could tie it for me, so he stood behind me tying the tie, both of us facing the mirror so that his arms were round my neck. He was chatting away about Mr. Lionel when to my amazement I saw in the glass that his hands had moved down from tying the tie and the next thing I knew they were under my hard shirt, stroking my body and feeling it. When I said, "Stop that at once," he took his hands away and looked quite discomfited, and he said, "I am sorry, sir. It was a misunderstanding. Mr. Lionel's friends always enjoyed it when I did that sort of thing for them," just as if he had handed me a delicious dish at dinner and I had refused it. Then he withdrew with dignity and a hurt expression.

There was a dinner party here and four others came. They seemed up to the standard of the occasion. Mrs. Templeton presided, wearing a diamond tiara as if she had been born with one on her head. After dinner we all bundled into cars and drove for miles till we reached an endless avenue and saw at the end of it Carborough Castle, where the dance was to be held. I was told that it is a copy of the renaissance Château de Chambord. It is enormous and many-turreted. Mrs. Templeton says it is "in appalling taste", but I thought lighted up against the night sky it looked like a castle in a fairy tale illustrated by Edmond Dulac.

Inside, we passed through one saloon after another hung with pompous portraits and furnished with splendid Louis xv commodes and consoles, till we reached the ballroom. There the dancing was well underway. I danced most of the time with Muriel, who is a good dancer but with an irritating habit of trying to lead. Felicity looked marvellous in a white dress covered with silver sequins. I had one dance with her. She danced most of the time with Basil. I must say they made a fine pair: he, very handsome; she, very seductive. After a time I began to feel tired and self-conscious standing by the door in my black tails when almost every other man in the room was in hunting pink. I told myself that it was a spectacle to watch the whirling couples under the chandeliers but I wished myself invisible. As the night went on the party got rowdier and all were stamping about the ballroom, bursting balloons and hallooing. I joined in, helped by five glasses of champagne, and got so hot that my hard collar went soft. A lot of the men had brought extra collars and went to change them when the first collar began to wilt.

When we got home from the ball we didn't feel at all sleepy. Muriel and I paired off, leaving Basil and Felicity together in the library. Soon we were kissing and mugging about in the drawing-room but when we came to I was horrified to see that my cigarette, which I had left burning in an ashtray, had fallen off and burnt a long scar in a magnificent Dutch marquetry desk. I said to Muriel that I would have to explain it to Mrs. Templeton, but she said, "I'll just move the lamp on top of the burn and no one will be any the wiser." By this time it was 6 a.m. and I was quite tired and feeling guilty about concealing the cigarette burn.

January 30
This morning when I got up I decided to tell Mrs. Templeton about the burn. She was very decent about it, although she did say that the desk was "rather a treasure". At breakfast Basil was in a very bad temper and bossy, and surprised me by shouting across the table to Muriel, "For Christ's sake, don't talk such balls," but she did not seem at all upset. She and I went for a walk in the rain and agreed to meet again in London. I caught the 11 a.m. train. Felicity decided to stay on for a few more days. In the train I read an account of the ball in a social column. It sounded marvellous. Although I would not have missed it, I don't know that I actually enjoyed it very much.

January 31
Sir Robert Borden, our former Canadian Prime Minister, is coming to Oxford shortly to make some kind of speech and will be staying at All Souls. I intend to call on him — he and my father were law partners, and great friends.

When I was still at school he wrote to me about the

Department of External Affairs in Ottawa, suggesting that it might be a career for me as he knew from my mother that I was interested in international affairs and he thought the Department would expand into a Canadian diplomatic service. I have this possibility in the back of my mind. It is true that in the last year or two I have lost interest in international affairs, but as a boy I used to follow them in the newspaper and make copious notes on them. Of course, I would have to get a good degree to get into the Department and also to pass their exams. I think I could do it. I have been working quite hard during the vacation and since this term began. But I do not write about work in this diary.

February 1
This afternoon I went to the Infirmary to see Jeremy. He looks less ghastly than he did just after the accident. He says that while in hospital he has made up his mind to go down from Oxford when he recovers and to look for a job, "perhaps something in the city". Although I shall miss him very much, I think he is right. He is quite unsuited to this place. He then began talking about Margot. He says he thinks that the only man she really cared about is Frankie Turner and that her husband realizes this and that is why he took her away to London for the Christmas vacation. He did not mind her sleeping around but does not want to lose her. While we were in the midst of this conversation, who should appear but Margot herself, armed with a bunch of flowers for Jeremy. She looked — for her — rather plain and chattered away in a very forced way so that Jeremy began to look exhausted. She and I left together and walked back into Oxford. When I said how much I missed seeing and being with her this term she first did not answer. This irritated me and I said, "There is no use in my talking to you when you are in this mood." She said, "It is not a mood, it is a fact — a fact that you could guess if you had any idea of anyone but yourself — the fact that I am

pregnant." I was stunned and must have looked my question, which was, "Who?" Before I could speak she said, "Now ask me 'Who?' It might have been a lot of people, mightn't it? But you need not look so scared, my pet — the ghastly thing is that it is my own bloody husband and he doesn't want me to have an abortion. He wants me to have the baby and he has taken a cottage in the country and we are to go and live there at any rate until the baby is born." "Oh," she wailed, "it will be such utter hell." I tried to console her. I could see she was on the verge of tears. When we got to the Iffley bus stop I said I would come with her on the bus, but she said no and jumped on the bus and we waved to each other as it took off. Shall I ever see Margot again?

February 2
Today I had a letter from Mother containing some wonderful news. Aunt Zaidée left more money than anyone expected. Not a fortune by any means, but it makes just the difference so that there is no need to think of selling The Bower, at any rate in the immediate future.

She also left me £200. I cannot help thinking what would have happened if I had had that money last term when Margot suggested that we should go to Paris together in the vacation. It might have changed everything. She would not have gone to London to join her husband and would not be expecting this baby. But would it really in the long run have changed anything? I have never really been in love with Margot as I was with Katherine. Yet Margot has made me very happy. I owe her a lot. Also, I am very fond of her, yet if I never do see her again, I'll survive!

Mother in her letter writes of next summer vacation and how lovely it will be for us to be together again at The Bower with Roley home for his school holidays. I am beginning to get quite excited at the idea of being back, which seems funny when I think how often I wanted to get away from Halifax. I feel I am a different person from the one who sailed for England last year but I don't suppose that anyone at home will even notice the difference.

EPILOGUE

Long after my Oxford days, when the house had passed into other hands, I returned to The Bower. In *The Siren Years* the scene is described as follows:

29 October 1940
I was thinking today of the last time I was in Halifax, Nova Scotia, and went for a walk to my old home, The Bower.

That day I was trying to look outward from an introspective bout of indigestion by reconstructing the road as it used to be. Only it was more a question of destruction than construction. First of all that row of white clapboard bungalows would have to be swept away and replaced by scrub and pine trees. Then over the stone wall of Gorsebrook — green fields must stretch to woods beyond where now hulked St. Mary's newly built Catholic College, in a monumental freestone, priests pacing its cement-filled paths. Where that stone wall ran my eye could detect the gap built in of new stones where had been a gate on which Peter and I had leaned on a summer afternoon, undirected sex driving us clumsy and breathless. In the Gorsebrook fields I had walked in my new beige Oxford bags reciting Rupert Brooke and trying to keep my pace steady when the small boys from the village catching sight of me through the gap called names after me.

The wall ended at the turn into The Bower drive. Here I was thrown back on memory with no stick or stone to help me — gone the gateposts, gone the lodge, gone the woods on either side of the drive and the tall trees that cast a green gloom until you came out on the slope which curved between rough lawns towards the house. I turned into the cul-de-sac of new houses which with their gardens had obliterated the former drive and woods. My walk was becoming an archaeological expedition, but instead of being buried under this new layer of living the old had vanished without a trace, swept off into space and time existing only in my memory.

There seemed to be an excessive number of dogs about. From each porch or garden gate of the new houses a barking dog bounded out sniffing my ankles. Children on bicycles circled the end of the cul-de-sac where The Bower house stood — for it still stood though crowded into a corner by the new houses so that it hardly had room to breathe. Shorn of its approaches it was at an awkward angle to the street. Altogether the house looked sheepish and out of place among its brisk new neighbours — too large — but without giving any impression of grandeur. They had painted it a musty pale yellow and torn down the vine from the front wall. All that was left of the lawns was a wedge of grass on which still stood the big oak tree. The house would, as they say, have been "better dead". Its physical presence there stopped the power of my imagination like a leaden block. I could not go into the house in my memory while that solid door stood facing me. Yet in that room above the porch on the left I was born. I had shivered and sweated out my adolescence. From that window I had watched for Katherine coming up the curve of the drive from under the summer green of the trees into the sunlight in her pink cotton dress swinging her straw hat in her hand.

But it was no use — these memories were manufactured.